What Is Psychology

The Science of You.
Simple, yet Powerful

Ghazwan Alemara

Contents

Introduction

Have you ever wondered why you think the way you do? Why certain situations make you feel elated, anxious, or even indifferent? Or perhaps why you make choices that sometimes surprise even you? Psychology holds the key to these questions and more. It's not just a field of study—it's the science of *you*.

The Science of You

In the simplest terms, psychology is the study of the human mind and behavior. But it's so much more than that. It is the lens through which we can understand ourselves and the people around us. Every thought, feeling, and action you experience has a psychological underpinning. Whether you're trying to improve your relationships, make better decisions, or simply understand why you feel the way you do, psychology offers valuable insights.

Why This Book?

This book was written with one goal in mind: to make psychology accessible and practical for everyone. You don't need to be a psychologist or have any background in the field to benefit from the science of the mind. This book will break down complex ideas into simple, relatable concepts that you can use to better understand yourself and others. Psychology isn't just for academics—it's for anyone who wants to unlock the secrets of human behavior and lead a more fulfilling life.

Why Now?

In today's fast-paced world, understanding human behavior is more relevant than ever. We face increasing challenges in maintaining mental well-being, navigating relationships, and managing stress. The ability to understand how your mind works can be a game-changer, helping you stay grounded in an ever-changing environment. From the rise of mental health awareness to the constant need for personal growth, psychology gives us the tools to thrive in a complex world. And this book will guide you through those tools in a way that's easy, yet powerful.

What You Can Expect

This book is divided into ten chapters, each exploring a key area of psychology, from cognitive processes to emotional regulation, and from the power of relationships to the science of personal development. We'll explore how your mind shapes your thoughts, emotions, and behaviors, and how you can take control of these processes to lead a more empowered life. Each chapter builds on the last, offering practical insights that you can immediately apply to your everyday experiences.

Tone and Style

This isn't a dense academic text. It's a simple, engaging exploration of what makes us *us*. The writing is conversational and straightforward, designed to be both informative and enjoyable. Whether you're a student, a professional, or simply curious about psychology, the content is tailored to meet you where you are. You'll find stories, relatable examples, and practical applications to keep you interested and involved.

A Journey into Yourself

By the end of this book, you'll not only have a better understanding of psychology—you'll have a better understanding of *yourself*. This book is a guide, offering you the tools to reflect, grow, and navigate the complexities of your own mind. So, get ready to dive into the science of you, and discover how simple yet powerful understanding psychology can truly be.

Chapter 1

Understanding Psychology – The Science of You

What Is Psychology Really About?

At its core, psychology is the scientific study of the mind and behavior. But that definition doesn't quite capture the full picture. Psychology isn't just about understanding how we think or why we act in certain ways. It's about uncovering the reasons behind the emotions we feel, the habits we form, and the decisions we make, whether we're aware of them or not. In essence, psychology is the science that explains what makes us *us*.

Psychology touches every part of our lives. When you wake up in the morning and feel that rush of energy or fatigue, when you make a split-second decision, or when you find yourself drawn to certain people, places, or experiences—these are all moments influenced by psychology. It's a discipline that helps us understand how we perceive the world, how we learn, and how our past experiences shape who we are today.

Psychology also goes far beyond individual experiences. It seeks to explain how we interact with others, how we form relationships, and how society influences our beliefs and behaviors. By understanding psychology, we gain a deeper understanding of not only ourselves but also the people around us and the world we live in.

One of the most fascinating aspects of psychology is that it evolves. As our understanding of the brain grows, so too does our knowledge of why we behave the way we do. Early psychological theories focused primarily on understanding the mind's most basic functions—like how we perceive light or respond to sound. Over time, these theories expanded to cover more complex aspects of human behavior, from emotion and motivation to memory and social interaction.

What makes psychology even more powerful is that it isn't just for scientists or researchers. It's for anyone who wants to better understand themselves and the world around them. Whether you're curious about why you get nervous before a big presentation, why habits are hard to break, or how people can form such different perspectives, psychology offers the answers.

In truth, psychology is about helping us live better lives. When we understand how our minds work, we can make more informed choices, build stronger relationships, and improve our mental well-being. The insights we gain from psychology give us the tools to navigate life with more clarity and purpose.

So, what is psychology really about? It's about you. It's about the people you care about. It's about understanding how we can all live more fulfilling lives by unlocking the mysteries of the mind.

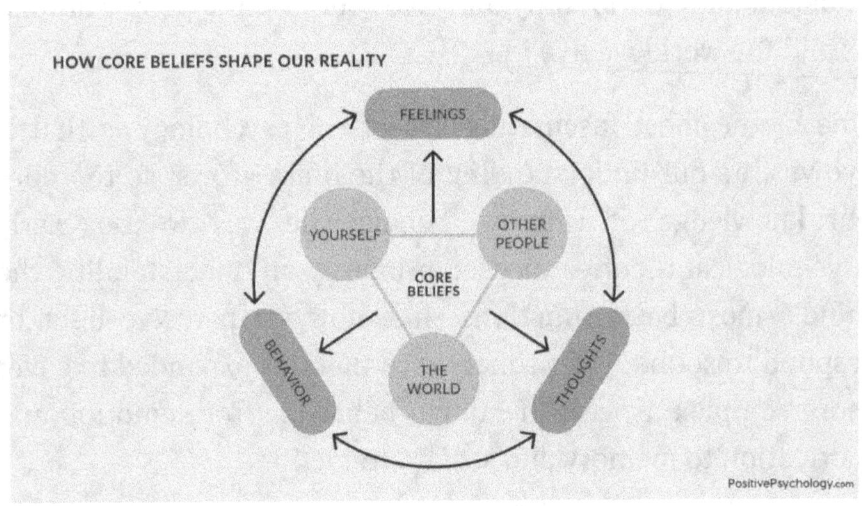

Psychology's Influence on Everyday Life. Source: linkedin.com

Why Psychology Matters

Psychology matters because it helps us make sense of the world—both the one around us and the one within us. At its core, psychology is about understanding why we think, feel, and behave the way we do. It allows us to decode the complexities of the human mind, and by doing so, it gives us the tools to navigate life with more insight and control.

Consider your everyday life. Each decision you make, every emotion you experience, and every interaction you have is shaped by psychological processes. From the way you communicate with friends and family to how you manage stress at work, psychology plays a role. Understanding these processes isn't just fascinating—it's incredibly practical. When you know why you react a certain way in stressful situations or why certain habits are hard to break, you gain the ability to change them.

But the importance of psychology goes far beyond the personal. Psychology is the foundation of many systems that shape society. In education, psychology informs how students learn and how teachers can better connect with them. In business, it drives effective marketing, leadership, and teamwork. Even in healthcare, understanding the psychological factors behind behaviors can lead to more effective treatments and improved mental health care.

Psychology also gives us the power to empathize. By understanding the mind, we can better understand others—why people act the way they do, why some struggle with mental health issues, and why relationships succeed or fail. This knowledge fosters compassion and patience, helping us build stronger connections with the people around us.

In today's fast-moving world, where we face constant demands on our time, attention, and emotions, understanding psychology gives us a crucial advantage. It helps us manage stress, improve our well-being, and make better decisions. It's no longer just about surviving; psychology shows us how to thrive.

In short, psychology matters because it empowers us. It provides a roadmap to navigate life's challenges with more confidence, clarity, and understanding. By learning how the mind works, you gain control over your own thoughts and actions, and that can change everything.

Psychology and You

Psychology is more than just a subject to study; it's a key to understanding yourself better. Whether you realize it or not, psychology plays a part in every decision you make, every emotion you feel, and every interaction you have with others. It's personal, practical, and relevant to your everyday life.

Think about the last time you had to make a difficult decision. Maybe it was choosing between two job offers or deciding whether to move to a new city. These decisions don't just come down to pros and cons. They involve your emotions, your past experiences, and even your personality. Psychology helps explain why certain choices feel harder than others and why we sometimes second-guess ourselves.

Or consider how you react when something doesn't go as planned. Some people are quick to brush off setbacks, while others might dwell on what went wrong for days. Understanding psychology can give you insight into why you respond the way you do and how to manage your emotions more effectively. This knowledge isn't just about getting by—it's about learning how to thrive.

Your relationships are also deeply influenced by psychology. From your closest friendships to your professional connections, psychology helps explain why some relationships feel natural and effortless while others take more work. It reveals the dynamics of communication, empathy, and conflict, and how improving your understanding of these can lead to stronger, healthier connections with the people around you.

But psychology isn't just about solving problems or analyzing your behavior after something happens. It's about building a greater awareness of yourself and using that awareness to live with more intention. When you understand how your mind works, you can make choices that align more with who you want to be, rather than just reacting to the world around you.

At its heart, psychology gives you the tools to be more mindful of your thoughts and actions. It allows you to recognize patterns in your behavior and understand what drives your motivations. This awareness is empowering. It helps you take control of your life in ways that bring more clarity, purpose, and fulfillment.

So, how does psychology fit into your life? It's there in the moments when you're trying to understand why you feel anxious about a new challenge. It's present when you're building new habits or trying to break old ones. It's in the way you connect with others and how you navigate tough situations. The more you understand psychology, the more you understand yourself—and that's a powerful tool to have.

Chapter 2

The Evolution of Psychology – A Journey Through Time

The Early Beginnings

The story of psychology begins with some of the earliest thinkers who were trying to understand the human mind and behavior. Long before psychology became a formal science, philosophers were asking the big questions: What makes us who we are? Why do we think the way we do? How do our minds work?

One of the earliest and most influential philosophers was Socrates, who lived in ancient Greece. He believed that by asking the right questions, people could uncover the truth about themselves. His method of dialogue and questioning, known as the Socratic method, was a way to explore thoughts and beliefs through conversation. This idea of questioning our thoughts is something that psychology still values today.

Plato, a student of Socrates, took these ideas even further. He believed that the mind and body were separate, and that our thoughts and knowledge came from the mind, not the physical world. Plato's belief in a "world of ideas" influenced how later thinkers understood the mind as something more than just physical processes.

Aristotle, Plato's student, had a different view. He focused on observing the world and believed that knowledge came from experience. This focus on observation and learning from the environment laid the groundwork for many of the ideas that psychologists would later explore. Aristotle's approach was practical—he wanted to understand how people learn, how they remember, and how they reason. His work is considered one of the earliest examples of psychology being used to explain human behavior.

For many centuries, ideas about the mind and behavior were largely shaped by philosophy and religion. It wasn't until the late 19th century that psychology began to emerge as its own discipline. This shift was led by Wilhelm Wundt, a German scientist who is often called the "father of psychology." Wundt believed that psychology should be studied like any other science, through observation and experimentation. In 1879, he opened the first psychology lab, marking the official beginning of psychology as a scientific field.

Wundt's work focused on understanding consciousness—how we experience the world around us. He encouraged his students to look inward, to examine their own thoughts and feelings as a way to better understand the mind. This method, known as introspection, was an important early tool in psychology, even though it would later be replaced by more objective methods.

These early beginnings laid the foundation for psychology as we know it today. Philosophers and early scientists like Socrates, Plato, Aristotle, and Wundt each contributed to the questions and methods that still guide psychologists. While their ideas were just the start, they opened the door to a deeper understanding of what it means to be human, and why we behave the way we do.

Freud, Jung, and the Unconscious

When we think about the mind, it's easy to focus on what we are aware of—our thoughts, feelings, and experiences that are right on the surface. But early psychologists like Sigmund Freud and Carl Jung believed there was much more happening beneath the surface of our consciousness. Their groundbreaking work on the unconscious mind changed the way we think about human behavior and emotions.

Freud and the Unconscious

Sigmund Freud is often called the father of modern psychology, and for a good reason. He introduced the idea that much of what drives our behavior isn't actually conscious but buried deep in the unconscious mind. According to Freud, our unconscious mind holds thoughts, memories, and desires that we might not be aware of, but they still influence everything we do.

Freud believed that the unconscious was like an iceberg: only a small part of it (our conscious thoughts) is visible, while the vast majority (the unconscious) lies hidden beneath the surface. He suggested that many of our actions, emotions, and decisions are shaped by unconscious desires and unresolved conflicts from childhood. This is where his famous concept of repression comes in—the idea that uncomfortable or painful experiences are pushed into the unconscious to avoid the discomfort they might cause in our conscious awareness.

One of Freud's key theories is that of the id, ego, and superego. He proposed that these three parts of our psyche constantly interact, often without us realizing it. The id represents our most basic instincts and desires, seeking immediate satisfaction. The superego is our internal moral compass, guiding us toward doing what is "right." The ego, caught in the middle, tries to balance the needs of the id and the rules of the superego. Much of this balancing act happens unconsciously, shaping our behaviors without us being fully aware of it.

Jung and the Collective Unconscious

Carl Jung, a Swiss psychiatrist who was once a close follower of Freud, expanded on Freud's ideas but took a slightly different path. While Jung agreed that we have a personal unconscious, he also introduced the idea of the collective unconscious—a part of the unconscious mind shared by all humans. According to Jung, the collective unconscious holds universal symbols, images, and archetypes that we all inherit and share, regardless of our personal experiences.

Jung's concept of archetypes is central to his theory. Archetypes are recurring symbols or themes that appear in myths, stories, dreams, and even in our everyday lives. Some common archetypes include the Hero, the Shadow (representing the darker aspects of ourselves), and the Wise Old Man. These archetypes, Jung believed, emerge from the collective unconscious and influence our thoughts and behaviors on a deep, often unrecognized, level.

While Freud focused more on individual psychological conflicts, Jung was interested in how these shared, universal elements shape our lives. He believed that understanding these unconscious archetypes could help people achieve a sense of balance and self-realization.

The Unconscious in Modern Psychology

Though Freud and Jung's theories have been debated and adapted over time, their ideas about the unconscious continue to influence psychology today. Many modern therapists still explore unconscious processes through techniques like dream analysis, free association, and even hypnosis, based on the idea that our unconscious mind holds important keys to understanding ourselves.

Both Freud and Jung believed that by bringing unconscious material to light, people could gain insight into their behaviors and emotions, leading to personal growth and healing. While their approaches differed, their shared focus on the power of the unconscious mind left a lasting impact on the field of psychology, shaping how we understand human behavior at its deepest levels.

In essence, the work of Freud and Jung opened up a new way of thinking about the mind. Their exploration of the unconscious brought to light the hidden parts of ourselves, revealing that we are driven by forces far deeper than what we can consciously grasp.

Modern Psychology

Modern psychology, as we know it today, has grown from a blend of scientific research, philosophical thinking, and practical application. Over the last century, it has evolved into a diverse and dynamic field, with psychologists studying everything from the workings of the brain to the behaviors of large groups. What makes modern psychology unique is its ability to explore both the inner world of the mind and the outward expression of behavior, all while applying scientific methods to get to the core of human experience.

One of the key shifts in modern psychology came with the rise of behaviorism in the early 20th century. Behaviorism focused on observable behavior, rather than thoughts or emotions, as a way to understand human actions. Psychologists like John B. Watson and B.F. Skinner believed that behavior could be measured and predicted based on stimuli from the environment. For them, psychology was about identifying patterns and understanding how people learn from their surroundings. Behaviorism laid the groundwork for much of what we know about habits, learning, and behavior modification today.

At the same time, another movement was taking shape: cognitive psychology. While behaviorists focused on observable actions, cognitive psychologists were interested in what was happening inside the mind—how people think, remember, and solve problems. Cognitive psychology gained prominence in the 1960s and 70s, thanks to thinkers like Jean Piaget and Noam

Chomsky, who helped uncover the mental processes behind learning, language, and development. This shift back to the inner workings of the mind allowed psychologists to explore new areas, including memory, decision-making, and attention.

Another major development in modern psychology has been the rise of neuroscience. With advances in technology, psychologists can now study the brain more closely than ever before. Neuroimaging techniques, like MRIs and PET scans, allow researchers to see which parts of the brain are active during different mental processes. This has opened the door to understanding how brain structure and function influence thoughts, feelings, and behaviors. Modern psychology is increasingly focused on how the biological, psychological, and social aspects of human life are interconnected.

Humanistic psychology also emerged as an important counterbalance to behaviorism and cognitive psychology. In the mid-20th century, psychologists like Carl Rogers and Abraham Maslow shifted the focus to personal growth, self-actualization, and the human potential for positive change. They believed that psychology should not only study what's wrong with people but also what makes life meaningful and fulfilling. The humanistic approach reminds us that while we can understand behaviors and mental processes, we must also consider the human spirit— the drive for purpose, happiness, and personal growth.

Today, psychology is more integrated and wide-ranging than ever before. Psychologists draw on a variety of approaches, combining insights from behaviorism, cognitive psychology, neuroscience, and humanistic psychology to get a fuller picture of the mind and behavior. Psychology is applied in countless fields—education, business, health care, and criminal justice, to name a few—and its influence continues to grow.

Modern psychology matters because it touches every part of our lives. Whether you're figuring out how to form a new habit, working through a mental health issue, or improving relationships, psychology provides the tools to better understand yourself and the world around you. The beauty of modern psychology is that it's always evolving, adapting to new challenges, and discovering new ways to make life better for individuals and society as a whole.

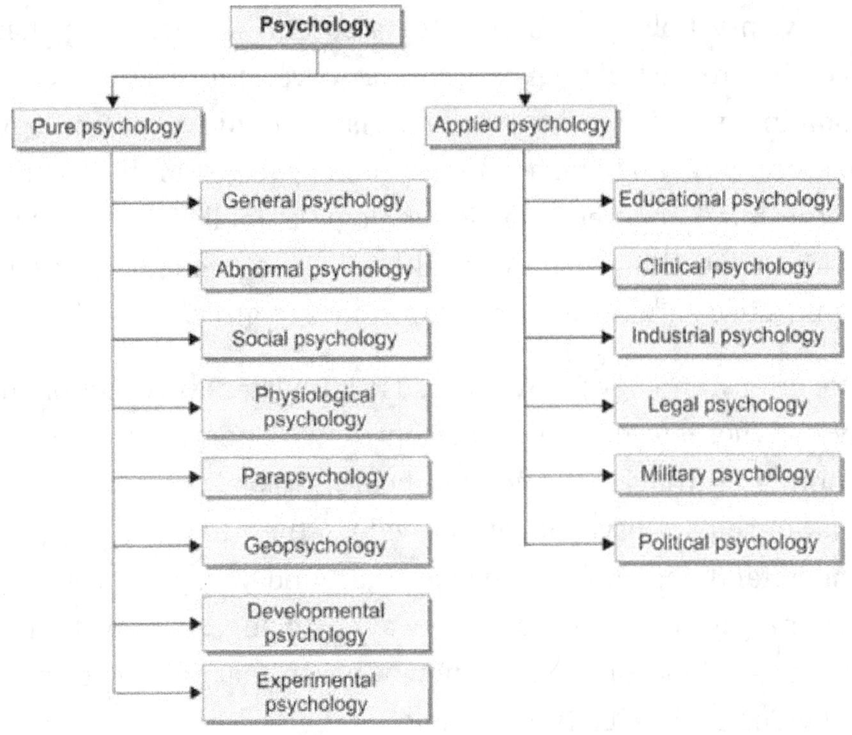

Branches of psychology. Source: jaypeedigital.com

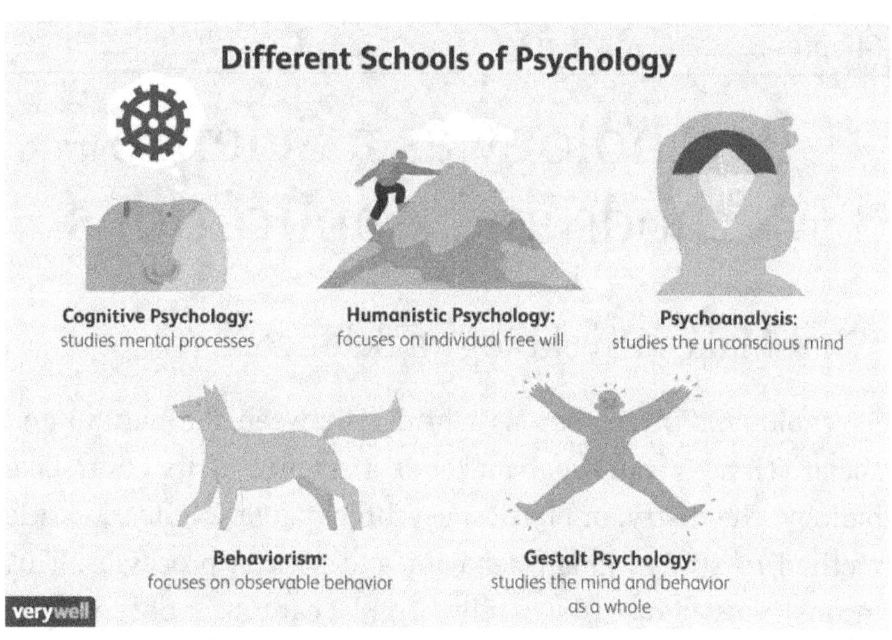

Schools of Psychology. Source: verywellmind.com

Chapter 3

Psychology as a Science – Methods and Applications

What Makes Psychology a Science?

Psychology is often seen as a bridge between the natural and social sciences, but what makes it a science at its core? Like biology, chemistry, or physics, psychology follows the scientific method to study human behavior and mental processes. This means psychologists rely on careful observation, experimentation, and evidence-based conclusions to understand how the mind works.

The Scientific Method in Psychology

At the heart of psychology's claim as a science is its use of the scientific method. This method involves several steps: forming a hypothesis, conducting experiments or observations, collecting data, and analyzing the results to draw conclusions. Psychologists, like other scientists, ask questions, develop theories, and then test those theories through research.

For example, a psychologist might be curious about how stress impacts memory. To explore this, they would first develop a hypothesis, such as, "High levels of stress reduce memory recall." Then, they might design an experiment where participants are placed in stressful and non-stressful situations, and their ability to remember information is tested. The results would either support or challenge the hypothesis, leading to a deeper understanding of the relationship between stress and memory.

Objective Measurement

One of the key elements of science is the use of objective, measurable data. In psychology, this means psychologists aim to measure thoughts, behaviors, and emotions in ways that are reliable and unbiased. Tools like surveys, brain scans, and standardized tests help gather data that can be analyzed objectively.

For example, when studying depression, psychologists don't just rely on a person's subjective experience. They use standardized questionnaires and clinical interviews to assess symptoms and determine the severity of the condition. This allows for a more consistent and scientific approach to diagnosing and treating mental health issues.

Replication and Peer Review

Science is built on the idea that experiments should be repeatable and that findings should be scrutinized by others in the field. In psychology, this process is essential for building trustworthy knowledge. When psychologists publish their research, other scientists review the work to ensure it's rigorous and free from bias. Additionally, studies are often replicated by different researchers to confirm the original findings.

For instance, if a study claims that a new therapy is effective in reducing anxiety, other psychologists might replicate the experiment with a different group of people to see if the results hold true. This helps strengthen the reliability of psychological findings and ensures they are grounded in evidence, not just speculation.

The Role of Theory

Like other sciences, psychology is driven by theories—broad explanations that help organize and understand complex phenomena. A psychological theory offers a framework for understanding behaviors and mental processes. These theories evolve over time as new research challenges old ideas and provides new insights.

Take, for example, cognitive behavioral theory. It proposes that our thoughts influence our emotions and behaviors, and by changing negative thought patterns, we can improve our mental health. This theory has been tested and refined through countless studies and has become a cornerstone of modern psychological therapy.

Balancing Objectivity and Subjectivity

While psychology is a science, it also deals with deeply subjective experiences. Emotions, thoughts, and behaviors are not as easily measurable as physical phenomena like gravity or chemical reactions. However, psychology bridges this gap by developing methods to study subjective experiences scientifically, using carefully designed experiments and statistical analysis to make sense of human behavior.

Psychology's blend of objectivity and subjectivity is what makes it such a unique science. It allows researchers to explore the intricacies of the human mind while grounding their findings in evidence, logic, and reason. Through this balance, psychology continues to evolve as a science, helping us better understand ourselves and the world around us.

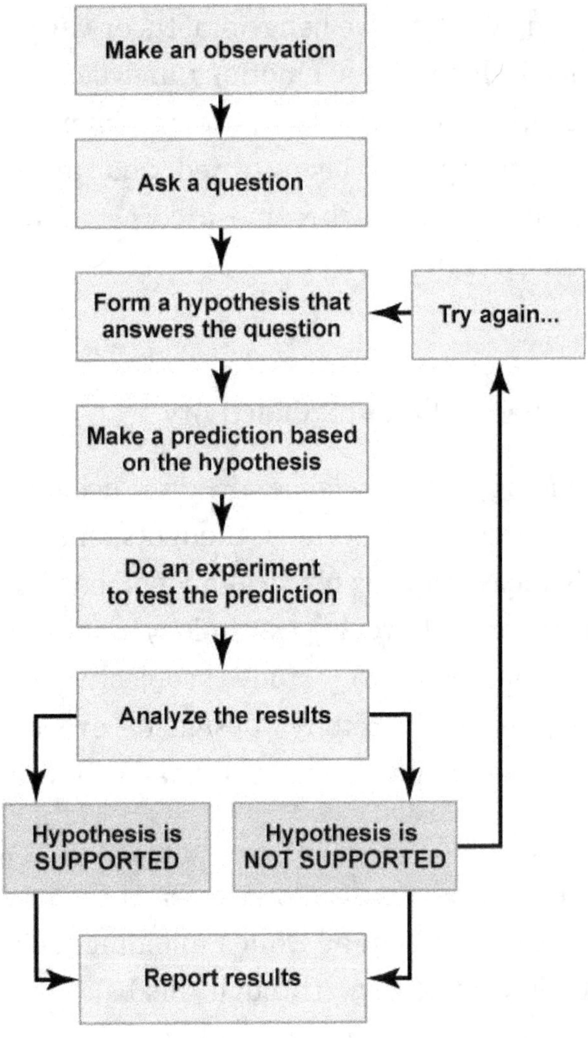

The Scientific Method. Source: pressbooks.pub

Experiments and Case Studies

In psychology, experiments and case studies are two essential methods used to understand human behavior. Both play a critical role in advancing knowledge, but they approach the study of behavior in different ways. Experiments allow psychologists to test specific theories under controlled conditions, while case studies provide in-depth insight into individual or unique situations. Together, they help paint a fuller picture of how the mind works.

The Role of Experiments in Psychology

Experiments are a cornerstone of psychological research. They allow psychologists to investigate cause-and-effect relationships by manipulating variables and observing the outcomes. In an experiment, researchers usually have two groups: an experimental group, where a variable is changed, and a control group, where the variable stays the same. This design helps researchers determine whether the change in the variable directly affects behavior.

For example, imagine a study designed to test whether sleep affects memory. The experimental group might be asked to sleep for eight hours, while the control group gets only four hours of sleep. The next day, both groups would be given the same memory test. By comparing their results, psychologists can see whether getting more sleep improves memory.

Experiments are valuable because they provide clear evidence about how one factor influences another. They are highly controlled, meaning researchers can isolate specific variables and limit the influence of outside factors. This control makes it easier to draw conclusions about what causes certain behaviors. However, because experiments are often conducted in artificial settings, like labs, the results may not always reflect how people behave in the real world.

Famous Psychological Experiments

Over the years, several psychological experiments have had a major impact on how we understand human behavior. One well-known example is the Stanford prison experiment, conducted by Philip Zimbardo in 1971. In this study, college students were assigned to play the roles of guards or prisoners in a simulated prison environment. The experiment was meant to last two weeks, but it had to be stopped after just six days because the participants quickly took on the roles in disturbing ways, with guards becoming abusive and prisoners showing signs of severe stress. The experiment highlighted how people's behavior can be shaped by the roles they are given and the power dynamics of a situation.

Another famous experiment is Stanley Milgram's obedience study from the 1960s. In this study, participants were instructed to administer electric shocks to another person (who was actually an actor) whenever they answered a question incorrectly. As the shocks increased in intensity, the participants could hear the actor expressing pain, yet many continued to obey the instructions to deliver the shocks, even though they felt uncomfortable. Milgram's experiment showed how far people are willing to go in following authority, even when it conflicts with their moral beliefs.

The Power of Case Studies

While experiments are great for testing specific hypotheses, case studies offer a more detailed look at individual or rare occurrences. A case study is an in-depth analysis of a single person, group, or event. This method is particularly useful when studying something that can't be replicated in an experiment, such as a unique psychological condition or a highly unusual life experience.

One famous example of a case study is the work of Sigmund Freud, who based much of his theory of psychoanalysis on case studies of his patients. One of his most famous patients was "Anna O.," whose symptoms of hysteria became the basis for Freud's development of his ideas about the unconscious mind and the importance of early experiences in shaping personality.

Another well-known case study is that of Phineas Gage, a railroad worker who survived a horrific accident in the 19th century when a metal rod was driven through his skull, damaging his frontal lobe. After the accident, Gage's personality changed dramatically, providing early evidence that different parts of the brain are responsible for different aspects of behavior and personality.

Strengths and Limitations of Case Studies

Case studies are valuable because they provide rich, detailed information about the individual or situation being studied. They allow researchers to explore complex issues that can't easily be examined through experiments, offering insights into the rare and unique aspects of human psychology.

However, one limitation of case studies is that their findings can't always be generalized to a broader population. Since they focus on a single case, it's difficult to know whether the conclusions drawn apply to other people in similar situations. Nevertheless, case studies often serve as a starting point for further research, helping psychologists develop theories that can later be tested in larger, more controlled studies.

The Balance Between Experiments and Case Studies

Both experiments and case studies are crucial in psychological research, and each method has its strengths. Experiments allow for precision and control, giving clear answers to specific questions about behavior. Case studies, on the other hand, provide deep insight into individual experiences that can't be captured in an experimental setting. By using both methods, psychologists can gain a well-rounded understanding of how the mind works, blending broad patterns of behavior with detailed individual experiences.

In psychology, the combination of experimental data and the rich detail of case studies helps researchers and practitioners alike uncover new truths about human nature, leading to more effective treatments, interventions, and ways of understanding ourselves and others.

Psychology in the Real World

Psychology isn't just something you study in a classroom or read about in textbooks—it's happening all around us, every day. From the way we communicate with others to the decisions we make at work, psychology plays a vital role in shaping our real-world experiences. Understanding how psychological principles apply in everyday situations can help us navigate life more effectively and make better choices.

Psychology at Work

In the workplace, psychology helps improve everything from employee performance to team dynamics. Managers who understand basic psychological principles can create environments that boost motivation, reduce stress, and foster collaboration. For instance, by recognizing what drives people—whether it's a sense of achievement, recognition, or personal growth—managers can tailor their approach to bring out the best in their team.

Psychology also plays a part in hiring decisions. Employers often use personality assessments or cognitive tests to evaluate candidates, ensuring they find people who fit well with the company culture. These assessments are based on psychological theories and help predict how someone will perform in a given role. Additionally, understanding the psychology behind leadership helps companies develop more effective managers who can inspire and guide their teams.

Psychology in Health and Wellness

Psychology has a significant impact on health, not just in treating mental illness but also in promoting overall well-being. Health psychologists study how behavior, thoughts, and emotions affect physical health, and they apply this knowledge to encourage healthier lifestyles.

For example, if someone wants to quit smoking or adopt a healthier diet, understanding the psychological factors that contribute to these habits is essential. Psychologists often use techniques like cognitive-behavioral therapy to help people change their thinking patterns and behaviors. This approach helps individuals not only address unhealthy habits but also build resilience and cope with stress in healthier ways.

Consumer Behavior and Marketing

When you walk into a store or browse online, the decisions you make are often influenced by psychological factors, even if you're not aware of it. Companies and advertisers use psychology to understand consumer behavior and tailor their marketing strategies. They study what grabs our attention, how we make purchasing decisions, and what drives brand loyalty.

For instance, the layout of a store, the colors used in advertisements, and even the placement of products on shelves are all designed with human psychology in mind. Marketers know that emotions play a huge role in buying decisions, and they use this knowledge to create more compelling campaigns. Understanding consumer psychology allows businesses to better meet the needs of their customers while guiding them toward making specific choices.

Psychology in Relationships

Whether it's your friendships, family ties, or romantic relationships, psychology is always at work. The way we communicate, resolve conflicts, and form attachments is shaped by psychological principles. For example, understanding how empathy works can help improve communication and strengthen your connections with others. Empathy allows us to understand another person's emotions, which leads to more meaningful and supportive interactions.

Psychology also helps us navigate conflict. Knowing how to manage emotions, avoid defensiveness, and listen actively can make all the difference when working through disagreements. Relationship psychology gives us tools to not only handle conflict better but also build healthier, more fulfilling connections.

Psychology in Education

In education, psychology provides insight into how students learn best. Teachers use psychological principles to design effective lessons, create supportive learning environments, and understand individual student needs. For instance, understanding cognitive development helps educators tailor their teaching strategies to suit the developmental stage of their students.

Psychologists also work with schools to address behavioral challenges and support students with special needs. By applying techniques like positive reinforcement and social skills training, psychologists help students overcome obstacles and succeed in their academic journey.

The Real Impact of Psychology

Psychology's influence stretches far beyond therapy sessions and academic research. It's a powerful tool that helps us understand human behavior in the real world. Whether you're making decisions at work, building relationships, or improving your health, psychology gives you the knowledge and strategies to live a more intentional and fulfilling life.

Chapter 4

The Mind in Action – Cognitive Psychology Simplified

What Is Cognitive Psychology?

Cognitive psychology is the branch of psychology that focuses on how we think. It explores the mental processes we use every day—things like memory, problem-solving, decision-making, and attention. Essentially, cognitive psychology is about understanding how the brain works when it processes information and how this influences everything we do.

Imagine you're solving a puzzle or making a choice between two options. The way your brain breaks down the problem, considers different possibilities, and eventually reaches a decision is all part of cognition. Cognitive psychology seeks to explain these processes in detail, offering insights into how we think, learn, and remember.

One of the key ideas in cognitive psychology is that the mind works somewhat like a computer. Just as a computer processes input (data) and produces an output (a result), our brain takes in information from the world around us, processes it, and then reacts in various ways. This field of psychology digs into what happens during that processing phase—what goes on inside our heads while we're thinking.

Memory is one area where cognitive psychology has made a big impact. Have you ever wondered why you can easily remember some things, like your best friend's phone number, but forget others, like where you put your keys? Cognitive psychologists study how we store and retrieve information and why some memories stick while others fade.

Problem-solving and decision-making are other crucial areas. Every day, we're faced with choices, both big and small. Cognitive psychology helps us understand how we weigh options, think through possibilities, and arrive at decisions. It also looks at why sometimes we make quick, instinctive choices and other times we take our time to think things through.

Another important concept is attention, which refers to how we focus on specific information while ignoring other things. Have you ever been so engrossed in reading a book that you didn't hear someone calling your name? That's your brain selectively focusing its attention on what's important and filtering out distractions. Cognitive psychologists explore how attention works and why it sometimes fails us—like when we're trying to concentrate but can't seem to stop thinking about something else.

Cognitive psychology doesn't just stop at understanding how the mind works; it also explores how these mental processes can be improved. For example, cognitive psychologists study ways to boost memory, enhance problem-solving skills, and improve decision-making abilities.

In essence, cognitive psychology helps us better understand the brain's inner workings. By exploring how we take in, process, and store information, it reveals the fascinating ways in which our thinking shapes every aspect of our lives—from solving everyday problems to making life-changing decisions.

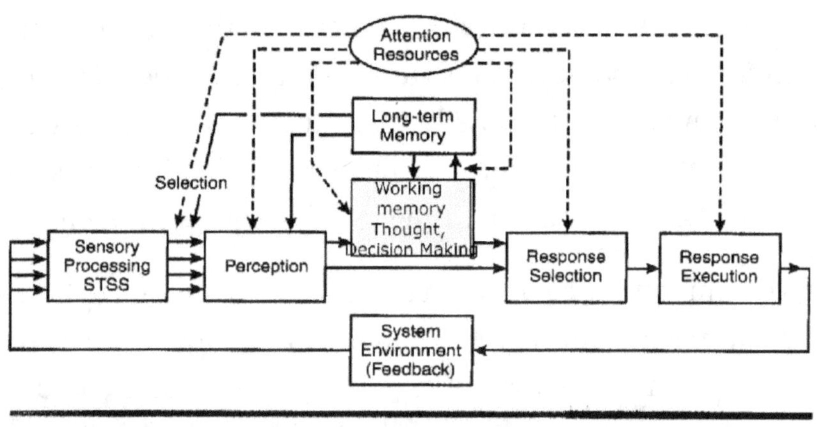

Figure 1.3   A model of human information processing stages.

How the Brain Processes Information. Source: stackexchange.com

How We Think and Learn

Have you ever wondered how your brain takes in information, processes it, and then helps you make decisions or solve problems? Thinking and learning are two of the most essential functions of the mind, shaping everything we do. While we often take these processes for granted, they are incredibly complex and fascinating.

How We Think

Thinking is the mental process we use to make sense of the world. It's the way we analyze information, solve problems, and come up with new ideas. When we think, our brain is constantly working behind the scenes, organizing information and helping us interpret what we see, hear, and experience.

One of the key ways we think is through patterns. Our brain loves patterns because they make it easier to understand the world around us. When we encounter something new, the brain tries to connect it to something we already know. For example, if you've never seen a particular type of animal before, your brain will try to relate it to animals you've seen before. This helps us quickly process information without having to start from scratch each time.

But thinking isn't just about recognizing patterns—it's also about problem-solving. Every time you face a challenge, your brain goes to work, weighing options, considering solutions, and predicting outcomes. Problem-solving can be as simple as figuring out what to eat for lunch or as complex as making a major life decision. What's amazing is how effortlessly we do it, even though the brain is processing multiple factors all at once.

How We Learn

Learning is closely tied to thinking. It's how we take in new information and make it part of our knowledge base. But learning isn't just about memorizing facts—it's about understanding and applying those facts in different situations. This is where the magic of the brain comes in.

The process of learning starts with taking in information. This can happen in many ways: through reading, listening, observing, or even doing. Once the brain receives new information, it tries to make sense of it. This is where thinking comes into play—your brain compares the new information to what you already know, looking for connections and patterns.

Learning is strengthened through repetition and practice. Have you ever noticed how the more you practice a new skill, the better you get at it? That's because repeated use of information or skills strengthens the connections in the brain, making it easier to recall and use that information in the future. This is why studying or practicing regularly helps improve performance—it's literally rewiring your brain to make learning stick.

Memory also plays a huge role in how we learn. Our ability to remember things—whether short-term, like recalling a phone number, or long-term, like remembering important lessons—makes learning possible. Memory allows us to retain information over time and access it when needed. But learning isn't just about storing facts; it's about being able to adapt that information to new situations, which is why understanding is far more valuable than rote memorization.

The Role of Attention

For both thinking and learning, attention is key. Our brains are bombarded with information all the time, but we can only focus on so much at once. Paying attention helps us select the most important information and ignore distractions. Think of attention like a spotlight, shining on the things that matter most and allowing us to process those details deeply.

The better we are at focusing our attention, the more effectively we can think and learn. This is why multitasking, though often seen as productive, can actually make it harder for the brain to fully process and retain information. By focusing deeply on one task at a time, we allow our brains to engage more fully with the material, leading to better thinking and more effective learning.

A Lifelong Process

Thinking and learning aren't just things we do in school—they're lifelong processes. Every day presents new opportunities to think critically and learn something new, whether it's through work, personal experiences, or even casual conversations. By understanding how we think and learn, we can become more intentional in our actions, making the most of the incredible capabilities of our minds.

Whether you're learning a new skill, tackling a problem, or reflecting on an experience, your brain is constantly at work, growing and adapting. The more you engage in these processes, the better you get at them, making thinking and learning some of the most powerful tools you have.

Mindset and Free Will

How much control do we really have over our actions? Do we consciously make choices, or are we influenced by forces beyond our awareness? These questions have fascinated both psychologists and philosophers for centuries. The concepts of mindset and free will help us understand how much of our behavior is driven by our own choices versus external factors.

Mindset: The Lens Through Which We See the World

Mindset refers to the attitudes and beliefs we hold about ourselves and the world around us. These beliefs shape how we approach challenges, setbacks, and opportunities. The work of psychologist Carol Dweck introduced two key types of mindset: fixed mindset and growth mindset.

With a fixed mindset, people believe that their abilities and intelligence are set in stone. They may think, "I'm just not good at math," or "I'll never be able to change." This way of thinking can limit their potential, leading them to avoid challenges for fear of failure. When you believe your abilities are fixed, you're less likely to take risks or try new things because failure feels like a reflection of who you are.

On the other hand, a growth mindset is the belief that abilities can be developed through effort, learning, and perseverance. People with a growth mindset see challenges as opportunities to grow, and they're more likely to persist through difficulties. If something doesn't come easily at first, they don't view it as a personal failure; they see it as a chance to improve.

Mindset matters because it influences how we view our choices and how much control we feel over our lives. When you adopt a growth mindset, you start to see possibilities for change and improvement. You feel empowered to take control of your decisions, believing that you have the ability to shape your own path.

Free Will: Are We Really in Control?

Free will is the idea that we have the power to make our own choices, independent of external forces. It's the belief that we are in control of our decisions and actions. But how much of our behavior is truly the result of free will? This question has sparked debate for years.

On one side, some argue that we have complete free will, that we make conscious choices based on our desires and intentions. Every decision we make, from what we eat for breakfast to what career path we follow, is seen as a reflection of our individual agency.

However, others argue that many of our actions are influenced by factors outside of our control, like our upbringing, environment, or even biological impulses. For example, habits we develop early in life can be hard to break, no matter how much willpower we think we have. Similarly, social pressures or unconscious biases can shape our choices in ways we don't always realize.

Psychology explores the balance between free will and these outside influences. While we may feel like we're making decisions freely, our minds are shaped by countless factors, some of which we're not even aware of. For instance, when we choose a particular career or relationship, we might be influenced by expectations from family, society, or cultural norms more than we realize.

The Intersection of Mindset and Free Will

This is where mindset and free will come together. While we may not have control over every aspect of our lives, our mindset plays a crucial role in how we exercise the free will we do have. When we believe that we can grow and improve (a growth mindset), we're more likely to make choices that align with our goals and aspirations. We take action, even when things seem difficult, because we believe in our ability to make progress.

On the other hand, if we have a fixed mindset, we might feel as though our choices don't matter much. We may believe that no matter what we do, we can't change our circumstances, which limits our sense of free will.

In the end, while external factors certainly influence us, our mindset shapes how we respond to these influences. By developing a growth mindset, we empower ourselves to make choices that reflect our true desires and ambitions, exercising our free will to the fullest extent possible.

Chapter 5

Emotions and Behavior – Why We Do What We Do

Understanding Emotions

Emotions are a powerful part of what makes us human. They shape how we experience the world, how we interact with others, and even how we make decisions. Whether it's happiness, sadness, anger, or fear, emotions are always at play, influencing our thoughts and behaviors in ways we may not always realize. But what exactly are emotions, and why do they matter so much?

What Are Emotions?

At their core, emotions are psychological and physiological responses to events or situations. When you feel happy, your brain releases chemicals like dopamine and serotonin that create a sense of pleasure and well-being. When you're scared, your body might tense up, your heart rate increases, and adrenaline surges through your system. These reactions are your body's way of preparing you to deal with whatever is happening around you, whether it's something positive or something that feels threatening.

Emotions can be fleeting, like a sudden burst of joy when you hear good news, or they can linger, such as when sadness sticks with you after a loss. They can range from mild to intense, and they can influence not only how you feel in the moment but also how you perceive and react to the world.

Why Do We Have Emotions?

Emotions serve an important purpose—they help us survive. Fear, for example, triggers the "fight or flight" response, preparing your body to react to danger. Happiness, on the other hand, reinforces behaviors that are good for us, encouraging us to repeat actions that lead to positive outcomes, like forming strong social bonds or achieving goals.

Emotions are also essential for communication. They allow us to express ourselves and understand the feelings of others. Imagine trying to navigate a conversation without being able to read the other person's emotions. Facial expressions, tone of voice, and body language all give us cues about how others are feeling, helping us connect on a deeper level. This emotional connection is crucial for building relationships and maintaining social bonds.

How Emotions Influence Behavior

Emotions are often the driving force behind our actions. When you're angry, you might lash out, say something you regret, or take immediate action to fix a problem. When you're excited, you're more likely to take risks or jump into new opportunities with enthusiasm. Emotions motivate us, whether it's to protect ourselves, seek pleasure, or avoid pain.

However, emotions can sometimes lead us astray. Strong emotions, especially when unchecked, can cloud judgment. We've all experienced moments where we've acted impulsively out of anger or fear, only to regret it later. Learning how to manage emotions, rather than letting them control us, is key to making better decisions and leading a more balanced life.

The Importance of Emotional Awareness

Understanding emotions starts with recognizing them in ourselves. Emotional awareness means being able to identify what you're feeling and why you're feeling it. It's not always easy—sometimes emotions can be complex, and we might not immediately know why we're feeling a certain way. But by paying attention to our emotional responses, we can start to understand what triggers them and how they affect our behavior.

Being aware of your emotions also helps you manage them more effectively. Instead of reacting impulsively, you can take a moment to assess the situation and decide how you want to respond. Emotional regulation—being able to calm yourself down when you're upset or pump yourself up when you're feeling down—is a skill that can be developed over time. It allows you to navigate challenging situations with more control and less stress.

How Emotions Shape Relationships

Our emotions play a huge role in how we relate to others. When we're emotionally in tune with ourselves, it becomes easier to empathize with the emotions of others. This empathy is what helps build strong connections, whether with friends, family, or colleagues. When you can understand and respond to the emotions of the people around you, you can communicate more effectively and create more meaningful relationships.

On the flip side, not being aware of your emotions—or ignoring them—can lead to misunderstandings and conflict. For example, if you're feeling frustrated but don't express it clearly, it might come out in ways that confuse or hurt others. Being open about your emotions, in a healthy and constructive way, helps prevent unnecessary tension and creates an environment where others feel safe to share their feelings too.

The Power of Emotional Intelligence

In recent years, the concept of emotional intelligence has gained popularity as an essential skill for success in both personal and professional life. Emotional intelligence is the ability to understand and manage your own emotions while also recognizing and influencing the emotions of others. People with high emotional intelligence tend to have better relationships, make more thoughtful decisions, and handle stress more effectively.

Developing emotional intelligence takes practice. It starts with becoming aware of your own emotions and learning how to regulate them. It also involves being attentive to the emotional cues of others and responding with empathy. By strengthening your emotional intelligence, you can enhance your ability to navigate life's ups and downs with greater ease and resilience.

Understanding emotions is key to understanding yourself and others. Emotions give meaning to our experiences, motivate us to act, and shape our relationships in profound ways. By paying attention to your emotions, learning how they influence your behavior, and developing emotional intelligence, you can live a more fulfilling and connected life.

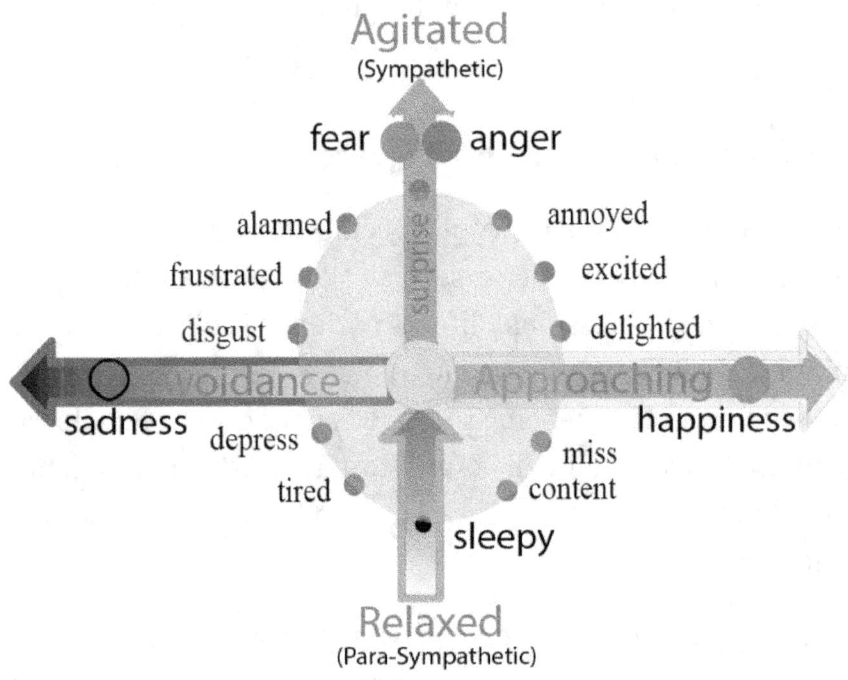

Emotions and Their Behavioral Responses. Source: researchgate.net

Behavioral Psychology in Everyday Life

Behavioral psychology focuses on how our actions are shaped by the environment around us. It explores how we learn new behaviors, why we develop habits, and how external factors influence the choices we make. Though it may sound academic, behavioral psychology is something we experience in our everyday lives, often without even realizing it.

Imagine you're trying to build a new habit, like exercising regularly or eating healthier. Behavioral psychology tells us that we are more likely to stick to these new habits if we are rewarded for them. If you give yourself a treat after a workout or feel the satisfaction of ticking off your goal for the day, you're reinforcing that behavior. This concept, known as positive reinforcement, is a cornerstone of behavioral psychology. It's why rewarding yourself for doing something good encourages you to keep doing it.

On the flip side, behavioral psychology also explains why some habits are hard to break. Let's say you're trying to cut back on sugary snacks. You may have developed a habit of reaching for a cookie every afternoon because it gives you a quick burst of energy. That feeling of satisfaction, even if it's short-lived, reinforces the habit. Breaking the cycle requires recognizing the reward and finding a healthier way to satisfy that craving.

Conditioning is another concept from behavioral psychology that we experience daily. It's the process of learning by association. Take, for example, why you might feel a sudden craving for popcorn when you sit down to watch a movie, even if you're not hungry. Over time, you've come to associate watching movies with eating popcorn, so one triggers the desire for the other. This is known as classical conditioning and was famously demonstrated in experiments by Ivan Pavlov, who showed that dogs could learn to associate the sound of a bell with the arrival of food.

Behavioral psychology also shows up in how we respond to others. Let's say you're at work, and you notice that whenever you compliment a colleague, they're more likely to help you with a task in the future. This is an example of operant conditioning, where behaviors are influenced by the consequences that follow them. If the consequence is positive, you're more likely to repeat the behavior. If it's negative, like getting ignored or criticized, you're less likely to do it again.

Even our motivations can be understood through the lens of behavioral psychology. Many of our actions are guided by a desire to avoid discomfort or seek out pleasure. If you've ever put off doing a task like cleaning or studying because it feels tedious, you're engaging in avoidance behavior. The immediate relief of not having to do something unpleasant feels rewarding, even though you know it might cause more stress later. Behavioral psychology helps explain why we procrastinate and how we can shift our behavior to be more productive.

In essence, behavioral psychology offers a powerful framework for understanding why we do the things we do. It teaches us that much of our behavior is learned through experience and shaped by the rewards and consequences we encounter. By becoming more aware of these influences, we can start to make more intentional choices in our everyday lives, whether that's building better habits, breaking unhelpful patterns, or improving how we interact with others.

The Role of Free Will in Behavior

One of the most fascinating questions in psychology is whether we are truly in control of our actions. Do we act based on our own free will, or are we simply responding to a series of external influences and internal impulses? Understanding the role of free will in behavior is central to understanding how we make decisions and why we act the way we do.

What Is Free Will?

Free will is the ability to make choices that are not determined solely by external circumstances or internal compulsions. In other words, it's the belief that we have the power to choose our actions, even when faced with difficult situations or conflicting emotions. This idea suggests that we are not just passive beings reacting to our environment, but active agents who can decide what we do next.

For centuries, philosophers have debated whether free will truly exists, and psychologists have taken up this question as well. Some believe that free will is an essential part of human nature, while others argue that much of our behavior is determined by unconscious processes or social conditioning. The truth may lie somewhere in between.

How Much Control Do We Really Have?

When it comes to everyday decisions, like what to eat for lunch or what time to go to bed, it can feel like we have complete control. However, research suggests that many of our behaviors are influenced by factors we aren't always aware of. For example, habits formed through repetition can become automatic responses, making it harder to exercise free will when faced with familiar choices. Similarly, emotions can drive us to act impulsively, even when we know a more thoughtful approach might be better.

On a deeper level, our upbringing, culture, and social environment shape our decisions in ways we may not always recognize. For example, societal expectations might lead us to pursue certain careers or relationships, even when they don't align with our true desires. These influences can limit the extent to which we exercise free will, as our choices may be constrained by outside pressures or ingrained habits.

That said, we are not powerless. Even when external or internal forces are at play, we still have the ability to reflect on our actions and make conscious decisions. This is where free will becomes important—while we may not have control over every factor that influences us, we do have the capacity to evaluate our options and choose how we respond.

Free Will and Responsibility

One of the key reasons free will matters is because it connects to the idea of personal responsibility. If we believe we have control over our actions, we are more likely to take responsibility for them. This sense of responsibility is essential for making ethical decisions, building relationships, and contributing to society. Without free will, the concept of responsibility would be much more difficult to define, as we would simply be acting out of reflex or necessity, rather than choice.

However, the idea of free will also comes with challenges. If we believe that we are fully responsible for our actions, we may struggle with feelings of guilt or regret when things don't go as planned. On the flip side, if we dismiss free will entirely, we risk feeling powerless, as if we have no say in our own lives. Finding a balance between recognizing the forces that influence us and embracing our ability to choose is key to understanding how free will shapes behavior.

Balancing Free Will and Determinism

Determinism is the opposite of free will—it's the belief that all actions are predetermined by past events or natural laws. From a psychological perspective, determinism suggests that every action we take is the result of prior experiences, genetics, or external stimuli. While determinism explains why certain behaviors might feel automatic, it doesn't completely rule out the role of free will.

Many psychologists and philosophers argue that both free will and determinism can coexist. For example, while we may be influenced by our biology and experiences, we still have the ability to make choices within those constraints. Think of it like walking on a path: while the road might be laid out in front of you, you still get to decide how you walk it, how fast you go, or whether you stop along the way.

The Role of Free Will in Growth

Free will also plays a significant role in personal growth. When we recognize that we have the ability to make choices, we become more empowered to change. Whether it's breaking a bad habit, learning a new skill, or improving relationships, free will gives us the power to take control of our lives and create positive change. Understanding how much control we actually have, and learning how to navigate the forces that shape our behavior, is crucial to becoming the best version of ourselves.

Ultimately, the role of free will in behavior reminds us that while many factors influence our actions, we are not just passengers in life. We have the ability to make conscious choices, take responsibility for those choices, and direct our own path, even when the road is filled with challenges.

Social Psychology – The Power of Relationships

What Is Social Psychology?

Social psychology is the study of how our thoughts, feelings, and behaviors are influenced by the presence of others. It explores the complex ways in which we interact with the world around us, from our close relationships to the larger society. While we might like to think we act independently, social psychology shows us that we are deeply influenced by the people and groups around us.

At its heart, social psychology is about understanding how social interactions shape who we are. For example, think about how you behave in different situations. You might act one way around your family, another way with friends, and differently again in a professional setting. These changes in behavior aren't random—they're shaped by social norms, expectations, and the people you interact with.

One of the key ideas in social psychology is social influence—how others affect our behavior, either directly or indirectly. We see this influence everywhere. It's the reason why we might dress a certain way to fit in with a group or follow trends because they seem popular. Social influence can be subtle, like feeling pressured to agree with the majority in a meeting, or more direct, such as when someone explicitly asks you to do something.

Another important concept is group dynamics. Humans are social creatures, and we tend to form groups based on shared interests, goals, or identities. Social psychology looks at how being part of a group can change the way we think and act. For instance, in a group, we might take more risks because we feel a sense of shared responsibility, or we might adopt stronger opinions when surrounded by like-minded individuals. This phenomenon, known as groupthink, can sometimes lead people to make decisions they wouldn't make on their own.

Social psychology also helps us understand conformity and obedience. Conformity occurs when we adjust our behavior to align with the expectations of others, even if it goes against our personal beliefs. This can happen in simple ways, like laughing at a joke you don't find funny because everyone else is laughing, or in more serious situations, such as following harmful trends. Obedience, on the other hand, refers to following the directions of an authority figure, even if it feels uncomfortable. Famous experiments, like Stanley Milgram's study on obedience, showed how far people are willing to go when instructed by an authority, even if it involves actions they wouldn't normally consider.

Beyond social influence, social psychology also looks at how we form impressions of others and how stereotypes and biases affect our interactions. When we meet someone new, we quickly form judgments based on their appearance, behavior, and even their association with certain groups. These judgments, though often subconscious, can affect how we treat others and how they respond to us. Social psychology seeks to uncover these biases and understand how we can become more aware of them in order to foster better, more equitable relationships.

In everyday life, social psychology is at play in countless ways—whether we're working as part of a team, navigating social media, or simply interacting with friends and family. By studying how social interactions influence behavior, social psychology helps us better understand the world we live in and how we can interact with it more thoughtfully.

Group Dynamics and Influence

Humans are social creatures, and much of our behavior is shaped by the groups we belong to. Whether it's a family, a group of friends, a workplace team, or even an online community, being part of a group affects how we think, feel, and act. Group dynamics—the ways in which people interact and influence each other within a group—can have a powerful impact on our decisions, behaviors, and even our sense of self.

What Are Group Dynamics?

Group dynamics refers to the patterns of interaction that take place when people are in groups. These patterns can be subtle or overt, but they influence everything from the decisions we make to the roles we play within a group. Group dynamics also involve the ways in which power, authority, and influence are distributed among group members.

One of the key features of group dynamics is the concept of roles. In any group, people tend to take on different roles based on their personalities, skills, and social standing. Some may naturally emerge as leaders, while others may take on supportive or passive roles. These roles often form quickly and can be difficult to change once they are established. Whether you're the one giving directions or the one following them, the role you play within a group affects your behavior and how others perceive you.

How Groups Influence Us

Groups can have a powerful influence on individual behavior. This is known as social influence, and it can take many forms. One of the most common is conformity, where people adjust their thoughts and actions to align with the group's norms and expectations. This can be as simple as following the dress code at work or as complex as adopting the political or religious beliefs of the group you're part of.

Conformity happens because we often look to others for guidance, especially in situations where we're unsure how to behave. In groups, the desire to fit in and be accepted is strong, so we tend to follow what others are doing, even when it goes against our personal beliefs or preferences. This desire to belong is so strong that it can lead people to conform even when they know the group is wrong—a phenomenon demonstrated in famous studies like Solomon Asch's conformity experiments.

Another form of influence within groups is called groupthink. Groupthink occurs when the desire for harmony and agreement within a group leads to poor decision-making. When groupthink takes over, people become reluctant to voice dissenting opinions or raise concerns because they don't want to disrupt the group's consensus. This can lead to flawed choices, as critical thinking is often sacrificed in favor of keeping the group united. It's why having diverse perspectives in a group and encouraging open discussions are so important for making better decisions.

Peer Pressure and Group Norms

Peer pressure is another way groups influence behavior. While peer pressure is often associated with teenagers, it can affect people of all ages. In groups, we feel pressure to conform to the norms and expectations set by others. These group norms can be explicit, like rules or guidelines, or they can be unspoken, like cultural customs or unwritten rules about behavior.

Peer pressure can be positive or negative, depending on the context. Positive peer pressure might encourage someone to take on healthy habits or try new things, like joining a fitness group or adopting a more productive work routine. Negative peer pressure, on the other hand, can lead to harmful behaviors, such as engaging in risky activities or abandoning personal values to fit in.

The Power of Authority in Groups

Another important element of group dynamics is the role of authority. Groups often have leaders or figures of authority who set the direction for the rest of the group. Whether it's a team captain, a manager, or a charismatic peer, the person in charge has a significant impact on how the group functions.

People tend to follow authority figures because they provide structure, make decisions, and reduce uncertainty. However, this can sometimes lead to blind obedience, where group members follow orders without questioning whether they're right or ethical. Famous experiments like Stanley Milgram's obedience study showed just how powerful authority can be in influencing behavior, with participants willing to perform harmful actions simply because they were instructed to do so by an authority figure.

How Groups Shape Our Identity

Being part of a group also influences our sense of identity. When we join a group, we often adopt the group's values, beliefs, and behaviors as our own. This sense of belonging is a key part of social identity theory, which explains how people derive a significant portion of their identity from the groups they are affiliated with. Whether it's a political party, a sports team, or a workplace, groups provide a sense of meaning and purpose that helps us define who we are.

At the same time, being part of a group can sometimes create divisions between "us" and "them." Group members may develop loyalty to their group and view outsiders with suspicion or hostility. This can lead to conflicts between different groups, as people become more focused on defending their in-group rather than collaborating or finding common ground with others. Understanding how group dynamics shape both cooperation and conflict is key to navigating social relationships.

Group dynamics and influence are present in every aspect of our lives, from the way we work to the way we relate to others. By understanding how groups affect our behavior, we can become more aware of the pressures we face and make more conscious choices about how we interact with the people around us.

Self and Identity

Who are you? It might seem like a simple question, but the answer is much more complex than it first appears. Your sense of self—your identity—is shaped by many factors, including your experiences, your relationships, and even the society you live in. Social psychology explores how we develop a sense of who we are and how our identity influences the way we see the world and interact with others.

The Concept of Self

At the core of your identity is your self-concept, which is essentially how you see yourself. It's made up of all the thoughts, beliefs, and ideas you hold about who you are as a person. For example, you might think of yourself as a caring friend, a hardworking student, or someone who loves music. These self-perceptions shape the way you interact with the world. When you see yourself in a certain way, you tend to act in ways that reinforce that identity.

Your self-concept isn't fixed. It changes over time as you grow, learn, and experience new things. Think about how you saw yourself as a child compared to now. You've likely developed new skills, interests, and relationships that have influenced your identity. Social psychology shows that our sense of self is constantly evolving, influenced by the environment around us.

Identity and Society

While we like to think of our identity as something deeply personal, it's also shaped by external factors—particularly by the groups we belong to. This is known as social identity, which refers to the part of your identity that is based on your membership in different social groups. These groups can be anything from your family, to your community, to the broader cultural or national identity you connect with.

Social identity plays a big role in how we relate to others. When we feel connected to a group, we tend to adopt the norms and behaviors of that group. This can be positive, providing a sense of belonging and purpose. But it can also create divisions, as we may begin to see those outside our group in a more negative light. Social psychology helps us understand these dynamics, allowing us to explore how our identity connects us with others and sometimes separates us.

The Role of Self-Esteem

Self-esteem is another important aspect of self and identity. It refers to how we evaluate ourselves—whether we feel good or bad about who we are. High self-esteem can give us confidence, motivation, and resilience. When we have a positive view of ourselves, we're more likely to take on challenges and pursue our goals.

On the other hand, low self-esteem can make us feel insecure or doubtful. It can hold us back from trying new things or cause us to compare ourselves unfavorably to others. Social psychology shows that our self-esteem is closely tied to how we perceive our identity and how we feel we're perceived by others.

The way we see ourselves is deeply influenced by feedback from the world around us. When we receive positive reinforcement—

like praise or support—it strengthens our self-esteem and affirms our identity. However, negative feedback or criticism can lead to self-doubt and insecurity. Understanding this relationship between self-perception and feedback from others helps us become more aware of how our identity is shaped over time.

Balancing Multiple Identities

Most of us have multiple identities. You might be a parent, a student, a professional, a friend, and a member of various social or cultural groups—all at the same time. Balancing these different roles can sometimes create conflict. For instance, you might feel torn between your responsibilities at work and your role in your family. Social psychology explores how we manage these different aspects of our identity and find balance in our lives.

Ultimately, our sense of self is a blend of who we are as individuals and how we fit into the larger world around us. By understanding the influences that shape our identity, we gain better insight into ourselves and our relationships, allowing us to live more authentically and meaningfully.

Chapter 7

Developmental Psychology – The Science of Growing Up

Psychology for Kids

Psychology isn't just for adults—kids experience the world in ways that are shaped by their own thoughts, feelings, and behaviors, too. Understanding psychology can help us see how children think, learn, and grow. It also helps parents, teachers, and caregivers provide the support kids need to develop emotionally, socially, and mentally.

How Do Kids Think?

Children's minds are constantly developing, and the way they think changes as they grow older. In the early years, kids are curious and eager to explore the world. Their thinking is often more concrete—they focus on what they can see, touch, and experience directly. As they get older, children begin to understand more abstract ideas, like fairness, time, and cause and effect.

Jean Piaget, a well-known psychologist, studied how children's thinking develops over time. He discovered that kids go through different stages of cognitive development. For example, younger children in the early stages might struggle to understand that others have different thoughts and feelings. But as they grow, they develop the ability to see things from other people's perspectives, which is an important part of learning empathy.

How Do Kids Learn?

Children are like sponges—they are constantly absorbing new information from the world around them. Learning happens in many ways, whether through play, watching others, or direct teaching. Kids learn by exploring, experimenting, and asking questions. They are naturally curious, and their questions help them make sense of the world.

Psychologist Lev Vygotsky believed that social interaction is a key part of how kids learn. He argued that children learn best when they interact with others, especially adults and more knowledgeable peers. When a parent explains how something works or a teacher guides a child through a new task, they are helping the child expand their understanding of the world.

Play is another powerful way kids learn. Through play, children develop important skills like problem-solving, cooperation, and creativity. Whether it's building with blocks, pretending to be a doctor, or playing a game of tag, kids are practicing real-world skills in a fun and engaging way.

Understanding Emotions in Kids

Just like adults, kids experience a wide range of emotions. They feel joy, frustration, excitement, sadness, and everything in between. But because their brains are still developing, they may not always know how to manage those emotions. It's common for young children to have strong emotional reactions, like tantrums, when they're overwhelmed or frustrated.

Emotional development in kids is all about learning how to understand and express their feelings in healthy ways. Teaching kids to recognize their emotions—like being able to say, "I feel mad" or "I'm sad because I can't play right now"—is an important first step. As kids grow, they learn to manage their emotions better, whether it's calming themselves down after a disagreement or sharing their feelings with a friend.

Parents and caregivers play a big role in helping children develop emotional intelligence. By modeling healthy emotional expression, like talking openly about feelings and handling stress calmly, adults teach kids how to manage their own emotions. Encouraging kids to talk about their feelings and validating those feelings, even when they're upset, helps children feel understood and supported.

The Social Side of Growing Up

As kids grow, their relationships with others become a central part of their development. Friendships are incredibly important for children. Through friendships, kids learn about cooperation, trust, and conflict resolution. They also start to understand social rules, like sharing and taking turns, which are essential for getting along with others.

School is often the first place where kids have to navigate these social rules on their own, without constant guidance from parents. This can be both exciting and challenging. Some children may find it easy to make friends, while others may struggle with social anxiety or conflict. Understanding how kids develop socially helps parents and teachers provide the right kind of support, encouraging positive interactions and helping kids navigate tricky social situations.

The Importance of Mental Health in Kids

Mental health is just as important for kids as it is for adults. Children can experience anxiety, depression, or other mental health challenges, even at a young age. It's important to recognize the signs that a child might be struggling emotionally. Changes in behavior, like withdrawing from activities they usually enjoy or having trouble concentrating, could be signs that something is wrong.

Providing a safe, supportive environment is crucial for a child's mental well-being. Encouraging open conversations about feelings and normalizing the idea that it's okay to ask for help when feeling upset or stressed can make a huge difference. If a child's emotional struggles seem to be more than they can handle, seeking help from a child psychologist or counselor can provide additional support.

Understanding the psychology of kids allows us to see the world from their perspective. It helps us support their growth in ways that are meaningful and effective. Whether it's helping them develop a sense of curiosity, navigate their emotions, or build strong social connections, a deeper understanding of child psychology can guide us in raising confident, happy, and resilient kids.

Stages of Life

Life is a journey, and as we move through it, we pass through different stages that shape who we are. Each stage of life brings its own set of challenges, opportunities, and growth. Psychology helps us understand how we develop at each point along the way, from infancy to old age.

Infancy and Early Childhood

The earliest stage of life, from birth to around age two, is a time of rapid growth and development. During this time, infants begin to explore the world around them, learning through their senses and forming bonds with caregivers. These early experiences lay the foundation for how we relate to others and the world later in life. Secure attachment to a caregiver is especially important, as it provides a sense of safety and trust that carries through childhood and beyond.

As children move into early childhood, typically from ages two to six, they start to develop language, motor skills, and a basic sense of self. This is also a period when they begin to understand social rules and the difference between right and wrong. Play becomes a central part of learning, allowing children to practice new skills and experiment with social roles. During these years, children's personalities begin to take shape, influenced by both nature and nurture.

Middle Childhood

From around ages six to twelve, children enter middle childhood, a time when their world expands beyond the family. School becomes a significant part of life, and children start forming friendships and developing their sense of independence. At this stage, kids become more aware of how they fit into social groups and begin to form their own identity based on their interests and abilities. They also start to grasp more complex ideas and take on responsibilities at school and home.

Cognitive development during this stage allows children to think more logically and understand cause-and-effect relationships. It's a time of curiosity and learning, where problem-solving and decision-making skills begin to take root.

Adolescence

Adolescence, which typically spans from the early teens to early twenties, is marked by significant physical, emotional, and psychological changes. This is the stage where individuals start to explore who they are and who they want to become. Identity formation is a major focus during adolescence, as teenagers experiment with different roles, values, and beliefs.

This period can also be emotionally challenging. The search for independence often creates tension between adolescents and their families, as they begin to question authority and seek their own path. Peer relationships become central, and social acceptance is highly valued. Adolescents may feel pressure to fit in or live up to expectations, which can lead to both personal growth and stress.

Young Adulthood

Young adulthood, typically from the twenties to early forties, is when people start building their careers, forming intimate relationships, and establishing their place in the world. For many, this stage involves making major life decisions, such as pursuing higher education, starting a family, or choosing a career path. It's a time when individuals strive for independence and stability, while also navigating the complexities of work-life balance and personal growth.

During young adulthood, individuals are often focused on achieving their personal and professional goals. Relationships, both romantic and platonic, take on deeper significance as people seek connection, companionship, and support in their personal and professional lives.

Middle Adulthood

Middle adulthood, from the forties to the sixties, is often a time of reflection. Individuals may find themselves evaluating their life choices and accomplishments, leading to what is sometimes referred to as a "midlife crisis." This stage can be a period of both personal fulfillment and reevaluation. For many, it's a time of caring for both aging parents and growing children, which can create a unique set of challenges.

Career-wise, people in middle adulthood may feel settled in their profession, or they may seek a new direction, wanting to pursue a different passion or interest. Psychologically, this stage is about finding meaning and purpose, whether that's through work, family, hobbies, or giving back to the community.

Late Adulthood

Late adulthood, from the sixties onward, is marked by significant life changes. Retirement often brings a shift in routine, and many people in this stage focus on enjoying the fruits of their labor or reflecting on the experiences of their lives. This stage is also characterized by reflection on legacy— what individuals have contributed to their families, communities, or careers—and how they want to be remembered.

Health becomes a central focus, as aging can bring physical challenges. Social connections remain important, and staying mentally and emotionally engaged is key to maintaining a sense of purpose and fulfillment. For many, this is also a time of wisdom and sharing knowledge with younger generations.

The Journey of Life

Each stage of life brings new challenges, growth, and change. Understanding these stages helps us navigate the journey with greater awareness and appreciation for the experiences that shape who we are.

Psychology in Education and Learning

Psychology plays a crucial role in education, helping us understand how students think, learn, and grow. It gives teachers, parents, and educators the tools to support students effectively, whether they are young children just starting school or adults pursuing higher education. By applying psychological principles, we can create learning environments that are not only more effective but also more engaging and enjoyable.

How Students Learn

At the heart of education is the process of learning, and psychology provides a window into how learning happens. One of the foundational ideas in educational psychology is that people learn best when they can connect new information to what they already know. This is why teachers often start lessons by reviewing previous material—our brains need those connections to fully understand and remember new concepts.

Different students also learn in different ways. Some might be visual learners, who understand material better when it's presented through images or diagrams, while others are more auditory, learning best through listening. Others still may be kinesthetic learners, benefiting from hands-on activities. Understanding these learning styles helps teachers tailor their lessons to meet the needs of every student.

Another important aspect of learning is motivation. Psychologists have found that students are more likely to succeed when they feel a sense of ownership over their education. When students are motivated by a genuine interest in what they're learning, rather than external rewards like grades, they are more engaged and tend to retain information better. Creating a learning environment where students feel curious and excited to explore new ideas can make a world of difference.

The Role of Memory in Learning

Memory is a key part of how we learn. Without memory, we wouldn't be able to store or recall the information we encounter in class. Educational psychology shows us that memory works in stages: we first take in information, then store it, and finally retrieve it when needed. Understanding how memory functions can help educators create strategies to reinforce learning.

For example, repetition and practice are essential for moving information from short-term memory to long-term memory. This is why students need to review and practice what they've learned over time. Techniques like spaced repetition—reviewing material at increasingly spaced-out intervals—are particularly effective for helping students retain information over the long term.

Teachers can also use psychological insights to help students overcome challenges with memory, like forgetting or feeling overwhelmed by too much information at once. By breaking lessons into smaller chunks and revisiting important concepts regularly, educators can help students process information more effectively.

Creating Positive Learning Environments

A positive, supportive classroom environment is one of the most important factors in student success. When students feel safe and valued, they are more likely to engage in learning and take risks, like asking questions or trying out new ideas. Psychology shows us that emotions play a significant role in learning—when students are stressed or anxious, it can be much harder for them to focus and absorb information.

Building a positive learning environment starts with strong relationships. Teachers who take the time to get to know their students, understand their individual needs, and show genuine care for their well-being create a foundation of trust and respect. This, in turn, encourages students to participate more fully in the learning process.

Psychological research also highlights the importance of growth mindset in education. A growth mindset is the belief that abilities and intelligence can be developed through effort and practice. When students have a growth mindset, they are more likely to embrace challenges and see failure as an opportunity to learn, rather than a sign that they aren't smart enough. Teachers who foster a growth mindset in their classrooms can help students develop resilience and a love of learning.

Supporting Diverse Learners

Not all students learn in the same way, and psychology provides valuable insights into how educators can support diverse learners. Students with learning differences, such as dyslexia or ADHD, may need additional support to succeed in traditional classroom settings. Educational psychology helps teachers understand these challenges and develop strategies to ensure that every student can reach their full potential.

For example, students with ADHD may benefit from more structured environments and shorter, focused activities that match their attention span. On the other hand, students with dyslexia may need additional time to process written material or may benefit from alternative ways of learning, like using audiobooks. By applying psychological principles, teachers can create more inclusive classrooms where every student feels capable and confident.

The Lifelong Impact of Education

Psychology reminds us that education is not just about passing tests or earning grades—it's about preparing students for life. The skills learned in school, such as critical thinking, problem-solving, and collaboration, shape how students approach challenges and opportunities long after they've left the classroom. When we understand the psychological principles behind learning, we can create educational experiences that help students not only succeed in school but also thrive in their personal and professional lives.

Ultimately, psychology in education and learning is about understanding how to best support each student on their unique journey. By applying these insights, educators can create environments that are both intellectually stimulating and emotionally supportive, helping students reach their highest potential.

Chapter 8

Psychology in Practice – Everyday Applications

Psychology for You

Psychology isn't just an academic subject or something that only therapists and researchers use—it's for everyone. Understanding psychology means understanding yourself better, which can have a direct impact on how you navigate your life. From the decisions you make to the relationships you build, psychology plays a role in every aspect of your day-to-day experiences.

Consider the last time you faced a challenging situation. Maybe you were feeling stressed at work, unsure how to manage everything on your plate. Understanding basic psychological principles, like how stress affects the brain and body, can help you handle these situations more effectively. Once you know what's happening in your mind, you can use strategies like deep breathing, mindfulness, or breaking tasks into smaller steps to reduce that stress and regain control.

Psychology also helps us make better decisions. Whether you're deciding on a major life change, like moving to a new city, or simply figuring out how to spend your weekend, understanding how your brain processes information can help you think more clearly. Psychology shows us that we often rely on mental shortcuts—called heuristics—that allow us to make decisions quickly but sometimes lead to mistakes. By recognizing when we're relying on these shortcuts, we can slow down and make more thoughtful choices.

Your emotions are another area where psychology offers valuable insights. We all experience a range of emotions every day, from joy and excitement to anger and frustration. Psychology explains how emotions work and why they're so important. When you understand your emotional triggers—what makes you feel happy, anxious, or upset—you can manage your reactions more effectively. Instead of letting emotions control you, you can develop emotional intelligence, which helps you respond in a way that aligns with your goals and values.

Psychology also teaches us how to improve our relationships. Whether it's with family, friends, or colleagues, relationships are at the heart of a fulfilling life. Psychology gives us tools to communicate better, resolve conflicts, and build stronger connections. For example, learning about empathy—how to understand and share the feelings of others—can help you see situations from another person's perspective, making it easier to connect and find common ground.

In everyday life, psychology can be your guide to understanding not just yourself but the people around you. It helps explain why people act the way they do and how you can navigate social situations with more confidence. By becoming more aware of the mental processes that shape behavior, you can approach challenges with a clearer mind and a greater sense of control.

Ultimately, psychology gives you the power to make more informed choices, manage your emotions, and improve your relationships. It's not just about understanding abstract theories—it's about applying those ideas to improve your life in practical, meaningful ways. Psychology is for you, and the more you learn about it, the more you'll discover how much it can enrich your everyday experiences.

Psychology in the Workplace

Psychology plays a vital role in the workplace, shaping everything from how employees collaborate to how they stay motivated and productive. Understanding the psychological principles behind human behavior can help create a work environment where people thrive. Whether it's improving communication, fostering teamwork, or enhancing leadership, psychology offers valuable insights that can lead to a healthier and more efficient workplace.

The Importance of Motivation

One of the most significant ways psychology impacts the workplace is through motivation. Employees who feel motivated are more engaged, productive, and satisfied with their jobs. But what motivates people? The answer isn't the same for everyone.

Psychological research shows that motivation can be intrinsic or extrinsic. Intrinsic motivation comes from within—people feel driven to perform well because they find the work meaningful or enjoy the challenge. Extrinsic motivation, on the other hand, is driven by external rewards like pay raises, bonuses, or promotions. While extrinsic motivators can boost performance in the short term, intrinsic motivation often leads to longer-lasting satisfaction and commitment.

Employers who understand what drives their team members can create environments that tap into both types of motivation. For example, providing opportunities for professional growth, offering recognition for a job well done, and giving employees a sense of ownership over their projects can all help boost motivation.

Effective Communication

Communication is at the heart of any workplace, and psychology can help us understand how to communicate more effectively. Whether it's between colleagues, managers, or clients, the way we exchange information affects productivity, collaboration, and the overall work atmosphere.

Psychology shows that clear, open communication builds trust and reduces misunderstandings. Active listening, where you focus fully on the speaker without interrupting, is a key component of effective communication. It not only improves relationships but also helps prevent conflicts and ensures that everyone feels heard and valued.

Nonverbal communication, such as body language and tone of voice, also plays a critical role in workplace interactions. Studies suggest that much of what we communicate is nonverbal, so being aware of how we present ourselves can make a big difference in how our messages are received.

Psychology can also shed light on how to give and receive feedback. Constructive feedback helps employees grow, but it needs to be delivered in a way that feels supportive, not critical. Understanding the psychology of how people respond to criticism can help managers frame their feedback in a positive, solution-focused way, leading to better outcomes.

Fostering Teamwork and Collaboration

Workplaces often rely on teams to get things done, and the psychology behind group dynamics plays a big role in how well these teams function. Effective teamwork depends on a balance of individual skills, clear communication, and a shared goal. But working in groups can also bring challenges, such as conflicts, misunderstandings, or the tendency for some people to contribute less when working in a team—a phenomenon known as "social loafing."

Psychologists have found that teams are more successful when they feel a sense of psychological safety—where team members believe they can take risks, share ideas, and make mistakes without fear of judgment or negative consequences. Creating an environment where people feel safe to speak up can lead to more innovative thinking and stronger collaboration.

Leadership also plays a crucial role in fostering teamwork. Good leaders understand the psychology of their teams and know how to bring out the best in each individual. By recognizing different strengths, encouraging open dialogue, and setting clear expectations, leaders can create a team culture that promotes mutual respect and cooperation.

Managing Stress in the Workplace

Workplace stress is a common issue that can affect employee health, well-being, and productivity. Psychology helps us understand the causes of stress and how to manage it effectively. High workloads, tight deadlines, or poor work-life balance can all contribute to stress, leading to burnout if left unaddressed.

Psychological strategies for managing workplace stress include promoting healthy work habits, such as regular breaks, realistic goal-setting, and time management techniques. Encouraging employees to maintain a healthy work-life balance and providing resources for stress management, such as counseling or mindfulness programs, can also help.

Creating a supportive work environment where employees feel valued and understood is another way to reduce stress. When people feel like they're part of a team and their contributions are appreciated, they're more likely to cope with stress in a healthy way.

Leadership and Management

Leadership is one of the most important areas where psychology intersects with the workplace. Effective leaders understand not only the tasks that need to be accomplished but also the emotional and psychological needs of their team. A psychologically informed leader knows how to motivate, inspire, and connect with employees on a personal level.

Different leadership styles can have a significant impact on workplace dynamics. For example, transformational leaders inspire and motivate employees by creating a vision and encouraging personal development. In contrast, transactional leaders focus on structure, rewards, and tasks. Understanding these different styles can help managers adapt their approach to the needs of their team.

Psychology also highlights the importance of emotional intelligence in leadership. Leaders with high emotional intelligence can recognize and manage their own emotions, as well as understand and influence the emotions of others. This skill is essential for navigating the complexities of workplace relationships and creating a positive, productive environment.

Understanding the psychology of the workplace allows companies to create environments where employees feel motivated, supported, and capable of doing their best work. By applying psychological principles, leaders can build stronger teams, foster better communication, and reduce stress, ultimately leading to a more productive and harmonious workplace.

Psychology for Health and Well-being

Health and well-being aren't just about physical fitness; they are deeply connected to your mental and emotional state. Psychology plays a crucial role in understanding how our thoughts, feelings, and behaviors impact our overall health. When we take care of our mental well-being, we can better manage stress, build resilience, and live more fulfilling lives.

The Mind-Body Connection

It's easy to think of the mind and body as separate, but psychology shows us how closely they are connected. When you experience stress, for example, your body reacts by releasing hormones like cortisol. In small amounts, stress can be helpful, giving you energy and focus when you need it. But chronic stress, left unchecked, can take a toll on your health, leading to issues like headaches, digestive problems, and even heart disease.

Understanding how stress affects your body allows you to take proactive steps to manage it. Techniques like mindfulness, deep breathing, and exercise are not just feel-good strategies—they're backed by psychology as effective ways to reduce stress and promote relaxation. By calming the mind, you can ease the physical strain that stress puts on your body.

Building Mental Resilience

Psychology also teaches us how to build resilience, which is the ability to bounce back from challenges and setbacks. Life is full of ups and downs, but how you respond to those moments can make a big difference in your well-being. People with strong mental resilience tend to view obstacles as opportunities for growth rather than insurmountable problems.

One way to build resilience is by shifting your mindset. Psychologists have shown that adopting a growth mindset—the belief that you can improve and adapt through effort—can help you face difficulties with a more positive and constructive outlook. This mindset helps you recover from failure and move forward, rather than getting stuck in negative thinking.

The Importance of Self-Care

Self-care isn't just about pampering yourself; it's a vital part of maintaining mental and emotional health. Psychology helps us understand that taking time to care for ourselves, whether through relaxation, hobbies, or connecting with loved ones, is essential for overall well-being. Engaging in activities that bring joy, relaxation, or a sense of accomplishment can recharge your mental energy and prevent burnout.

Self-care also includes setting boundaries. Learning to say no when necessary, managing your workload, and protecting your personal time are crucial psychological strategies for maintaining a healthy balance between work and life.

Mental Health and Support

Psychology is at the forefront of mental health treatment, offering tools to address anxiety, depression, and other mental health challenges. If you ever feel overwhelmed, it's important to recognize that reaching out for support—whether from a psychologist, counselor, or trusted friend—is a strength, not a weakness.

Therapies like cognitive-behavioral therapy (CBT) have been proven to help people change unhelpful thought patterns and behaviors. Whether you're dealing with stress, anxiety, or emotional challenges, psychology offers practical approaches that can guide you toward better mental health. These therapies teach coping mechanisms that can be used in everyday life to help manage difficult emotions and thoughts.

Living a Balanced Life

Incorporating psychology into your approach to health and well-being means making intentional choices that benefit both your mind and body. It's about recognizing when your mental health needs attention and taking steps to nurture it, just as you would care for your physical health. By understanding the psychological factors that affect your well-being, you can create a lifestyle that supports both mental and physical health, leading to a happier, more balanced life.

Chapter 9

The Psychology of Exceptional Minds

What Is Psychology for Exceptional Children?

Psychology for exceptional children focuses on understanding and supporting kids who have unique developmental, intellectual, or emotional needs. These children may have disabilities, such as learning difficulties or autism, or they may be gifted and talented in certain areas. In both cases, psychology plays a critical role in helping them reach their full potential by recognizing their strengths, addressing their challenges, and providing the right environment for growth.

Understanding Exceptional Children

Every child is different, but exceptional children stand out in one or more areas of development. Some may excel academically or artistically, while others may face difficulties in learning, socializing, or managing emotions. Psychologists who work with exceptional children aim to understand their individual needs and create tailored approaches to support their development.

For children with disabilities, psychologists look for ways to help them overcome challenges and thrive in everyday life. This could involve strategies to improve learning, communication, or social skills. For gifted children, the goal is often to challenge them in ways that keep them engaged and excited about learning, while also helping them navigate the social and emotional complexities that sometimes come with being ahead of their peers.

The Role of Assessment

One of the key tools in psychology for exceptional children is assessment. Psychologists use a variety of tests and observations to understand a child's abilities, strengths, and areas where they may need support. These assessments help identify learning disabilities, such as dyslexia or ADHD, or areas where a child may excel, like advanced math or creative problem-solving.

Assessment is not just about labeling a child—it's about providing a roadmap for how best to support them. Once a psychologist understands a child's unique profile, they can recommend interventions, therapies, or specialized educational plans to help the child succeed.

Support for Learning Disabilities

Children with learning disabilities often struggle in traditional classroom settings because their brains process information differently. Psychology helps educators and parents understand these differences and find ways to teach that align with the child's learning style. For example, a child with dyslexia might benefit from reading programs that break down words into smaller, more manageable parts, while a child with ADHD might do better in an environment that allows for more movement and flexibility.

Psychologists also work with children to develop coping strategies for the challenges they face. This might include teaching them ways to stay organized, manage frustration, or build self-confidence, so they can approach learning with a positive attitude.

Supporting Gifted Children

Gifted children have their own set of challenges. While they may excel academically, they sometimes struggle with boredom in the classroom or feel isolated from their peers who don't share their interests. Psychologists help gifted children find ways to stay challenged and engaged in their education, whether that means accelerating through certain subjects, participating in specialized programs, or pursuing extracurricular activities that match their passions.

Gifted children can also experience social and emotional challenges, such as perfectionism, anxiety, or difficulty relating to others. Psychology offers tools to help them navigate these feelings, build resilience, and develop healthy relationships with peers and adults.

Creating Inclusive Environments

For both children with disabilities and gifted children, the goal of psychology is to create inclusive environments where they can succeed. This often involves collaboration between psychologists, teachers, and parents to ensure that the child's educational and emotional needs are being met. An inclusive environment recognizes that every child learns differently and that those differences should be embraced, not seen as obstacles.

In schools, this might mean offering individualized education plans (IEPs) for children with disabilities or providing opportunities for gifted students to work at their own pace. At home, it means creating a supportive and understanding atmosphere where children feel valued for who they are, regardless of their challenges or talents.

Fostering Growth and Confidence

Ultimately, psychology for exceptional children is about helping them grow into confident, capable individuals. Whether a child has a disability or is gifted, the right support can make a world of difference. By understanding their unique needs and providing tailored strategies, psychologists help children develop the skills they need to succeed academically, socially, and emotionally.

Every child deserves the opportunity to reach their full potential, and psychology is key to unlocking that potential for exceptional children. It provides the tools and insights needed to create supportive environments that encourage learning, creativity, and personal growth.

Psychology and Criminology

Psychology and criminology intersect in fascinating ways, providing insight into why people commit crimes and how we can prevent criminal behavior. Criminology focuses on understanding crime and its effects on society, while psychology looks at the individual—their thoughts, emotions, and actions. Together, these fields help us explore the psychological factors that contribute to criminal behavior and how society responds to crime.

Understanding Criminal Behavior

One of the key questions psychology addresses in criminology is: why do people break the law? While there is no single answer, psychologists have identified several factors that can influence criminal behavior. These can range from environmental influences, like poverty or peer pressure, to individual factors such as personality traits, mental health issues, or a history of trauma.

For instance, some people may engage in criminal activities because of learned behaviors. This is where behavioral psychology comes into play. If someone grows up in an environment where crime is normalized or even rewarded, they might learn that breaking the law is an acceptable way to achieve certain goals. This concept, known as social learning theory, explains how behavior is often shaped by observing and imitating others, especially in formative years.

In addition to learned behaviors, personality traits play a significant role. Traits such as impulsivity, aggression, or a lack of empathy are often linked to criminal behavior. Psychologists who study these traits work to understand how they develop and how they can be addressed to reduce the likelihood of criminal actions.

Mental Health and Crime

Mental health issues can also contribute to criminal behavior. People suffering from disorders like schizophrenia, bipolar disorder, or severe depression may engage in illegal activities, sometimes as a result of their condition. For example, someone experiencing a psychotic episode might commit a crime they wouldn't otherwise consider when in a stable mental state.

However, it's important to note that most people with mental health issues are not criminals, and they are more likely to be victims than perpetrators. Still, understanding the role mental health can play in criminal behavior helps the legal system treat individuals with compassion and direct them toward the right support, such as rehabilitation or mental health services.

The Criminal Mind

One area where psychology has made a significant impact on criminology is in profiling criminal behavior, particularly for violent crimes. Criminal profiling is used to identify patterns of behavior that might point to a suspect's personality or motives.

This is especially useful in cases involving serial crimes, where understanding the psychological makeup of the perpetrator can help investigators predict future actions or identify them before they strike again.

Forensic psychologists also work within the legal system to assess individuals involved in crimes. They might evaluate a defendant's mental state to determine if they are fit to stand trial, or they may assess the likelihood of reoffending. In some cases, forensic psychologists work directly with offenders to develop treatment plans aimed at rehabilitation rather than punishment.

Prevention and Rehabilitation

The ultimate goal of combining psychology with criminology is not only to understand crime but also to prevent it. By identifying risk factors—such as a lack of emotional support, exposure to violence, or untreated mental illness—psychologists can help create programs that steer people away from criminal paths.

Rehabilitation is another key focus. Instead of simply punishing offenders, psychology-based rehabilitation programs aim to address the underlying psychological issues that contribute to criminal behavior. Whether through therapy, education, or support in finding stable employment, these programs help reduce the likelihood of reoffending and promote reintegration into society.

Psychology and criminology together offer a deeper understanding of crime by looking beyond the act itself to explore the human mind behind it. This approach allows for more compassionate, effective ways to address and prevent crime, benefiting both individuals and society.

Near-Death Experiences and Psychology

Near-death experiences (NDEs) have fascinated people for centuries. These are the profound and often life-changing events that occur when a person comes close to death or is in a life-threatening situation. Many people who have had NDEs describe sensations like floating above their body, seeing a bright light, or feeling an overwhelming sense of peace. While these experiences can be deeply personal and spiritual, psychology offers insight into why and how they happen.

What Happens During a Near-Death Experience?

Near-death experiences often occur when someone has a close brush with death, such as during a serious accident, cardiac arrest, or intense medical situation. Those who experience NDEs frequently report similar phenomena: a sense of detachment from their physical body, a feeling of moving through a tunnel, encounters with deceased loved ones, and sometimes even a review of their life.

Psychologists have studied these common elements and found that NDEs seem to follow certain patterns, regardless of a person's cultural or religious background. While the specifics of the experience can vary, the general themes—like the sense of peace or the bright light—are surprisingly consistent.

The Brain and Near-Death Experiences

One of the key questions psychologists explore is whether NDEs are the result of physiological processes in the brain. When a person is near death, their brain may be deprived of oxygen or flooded with stress hormones, both of which can affect how they perceive reality. Some researchers suggest that the feeling of leaving the body could be the brain's way of responding to extreme stress or trauma. The tunnel and bright light, which are commonly reported, may be linked to changes in brain activity as it starts to shut down.

While these explanations offer a scientific perspective on NDEs, they don't fully account for the emotional and psychological impact these experiences have on those who live through them. Many people describe their NDEs as transformative, changing the way they view life, death, and their sense of purpose.

The Psychological Impact of NDEs

For many, a near-death experience leads to significant changes in how they live their lives. Some report feeling less afraid of death, believing that there is something beyond this life. Others describe a renewed sense of purpose, feeling that they have been given a second chance to make the most of their time on Earth. These psychological shifts can be powerful, leading to changes in relationships, career paths, and personal priorities.

However, not all NDEs are entirely positive. Some people experience distressing or frightening near-death experiences, which can leave them with feelings of anxiety or confusion about what they went through. In these cases, psychologists often play a role in helping individuals process their experience and come to terms with the emotional aftermath.

Exploring the Meaning of NDEs

Psychologists don't just look at the biological aspects of near-death experiences; they also explore their psychological and emotional significance. For many, an NDE can be a deeply meaningful event that reshapes their understanding of life and death. These experiences often challenge people's existing beliefs, and processing the meaning of an NDE can take time.

Some psychologists see NDEs as part of the mind's attempt to make sense of a life-threatening event. The experience may serve as a psychological coping mechanism, helping the person deal with the fear and uncertainty of being close to death. Others view NDEs as a way for individuals to tap into a deeper part of their consciousness, one that is not usually accessible in everyday life.

The Ongoing Mystery of NDEs

Despite decades of research, near-death experiences remain a mystery in many ways. Psychology offers valuable insights into how the brain might contribute to these experiences, but the profound emotional and spiritual impact of NDEs suggests that there is still much to learn. Whether an NDE is seen as a purely psychological event or something more, it is clear that these experiences can have a lasting and meaningful impact on those who go through them.

For individuals who have experienced a near-death event, psychology provides tools to help them process and understand what they've gone through. And for the rest of us, studying NDEs can offer a fascinating glimpse into the intersection of life, death, and the human mind.

Chapter 10

Future Directions in Psychology – What's Next?

Emerging Trends in Psychology

Psychology is always evolving, and new trends continue to shape the field as our understanding of the human mind grows and technology advances. These emerging trends reflect shifts in how we approach mental health, behavior, and the mind-body connection. As society changes, so does the focus of psychological research and practice. Here are some of the most exciting and influential trends shaping the future of psychology.

The Rise of Digital Mental Health

One of the biggest shifts in psychology today is the integration of digital tools into mental health care. With the rise of smartphones, apps, and online platforms, mental health services are becoming more accessible than ever before. Teletherapy, where patients can speak to a therapist via video or phone, has made it easier for people to receive support from the comfort of their own homes. This has been particularly valuable for individuals in remote areas or those with limited access to traditional therapy.

In addition to teletherapy, mental health apps have gained popularity for helping people manage anxiety, depression, and stress. These apps offer a range of tools, from mindfulness exercises to mood tracking, and are often used as a supplement to in-person therapy. As digital health continues to grow, the future of mental health care may increasingly blend face-to-face interactions with technology-driven solutions.

Focus on Mental Health in the Workplace

In recent years, there has been a growing recognition of the importance of mental health in the workplace. Employers are beginning to realize that a healthy workforce is not just about physical health but mental well-being as well. As a result, more organizations are investing in mental health programs, offering services such as counseling, stress management workshops, and wellness initiatives.

Psychologists are also working with companies to create healthier work environments that reduce burnout and promote mental health. This includes strategies to manage workload, foster work-life balance, and create supportive cultures where employees feel valued. The shift toward prioritizing mental health at work reflects a broader understanding that well-being is central to productivity and job satisfaction.

Neuropsychology and Brain Imaging

Advances in neuroscience have opened up new avenues for understanding how the brain influences behavior. Neuropsychology, which studies the relationship between brain function and behavior, has grown rapidly with the help of brain imaging technologies like fMRI and PET scans. These tools allow researchers to observe brain activity in real time, giving them a better understanding of how different parts of the brain contribute to emotions, memory, decision-making, and more.

The use of neuroimaging is particularly important in areas like mental health, where it can help identify the neurological underpinnings of disorders such as depression, anxiety, or schizophrenia. It also provides insights into how the brain changes with therapy, allowing psychologists to develop more targeted treatments. As brain imaging technology continues to advance, the field of neuropsychology will likely play an even bigger role in both research and clinical practice.

The Growing Interest in Positive Psychology

While much of psychology traditionally focused on diagnosing and treating mental illness, there has been a growing interest in studying what makes life fulfilling and meaningful. Positive psychology is the branch of psychology that explores human strengths, well-being, and happiness. Rather than focusing solely on what goes wrong, positive psychology looks at what helps people thrive.

Researchers in this field study topics like gratitude, resilience, and purpose, seeking to understand how these qualities contribute to a good life. The goal of positive psychology is not only to help people overcome difficulties but to enable them to flourish by building on their strengths. This trend reflects a more holistic approach to mental health, one that emphasizes personal growth and well-being in addition to symptom reduction.

Psychology and Social Justice

Another emerging trend is the increased focus on social justice within psychology. Psychologists are becoming more aware of how social, cultural, and economic factors influence mental health. This includes recognizing the impact of systemic issues like racism, inequality, and discrimination on individuals and communities. There is a growing emphasis on making mental health care more inclusive and accessible to marginalized populations.

This trend has led to greater advocacy for mental health policies that address disparities in care and promote equity. Psychologists are also working to incorporate culturally sensitive practices into their work, ensuring that treatment approaches respect the diverse backgrounds and experiences of their clients. As the world becomes more interconnected and diverse, psychology is evolving to better meet the needs of all individuals, regardless of their background or circumstances.

Integrating Mindfulness and Holistic Approaches

Mindfulness and holistic practices are becoming increasingly popular in both clinical and everyday settings. Mindfulness, the practice of staying present and aware of the moment without judgment, has been shown to reduce stress, improve focus, and enhance emotional regulation. It is often used in therapies like Mindfulness-Based Stress Reduction (MBSR) and Mindfulness-Based Cognitive Therapy (MBCT) to help individuals manage anxiety, depression, and chronic pain.

Holistic approaches, which consider the whole person—mind, body, and spirit—are gaining traction in mental health care. These approaches often combine traditional psychological techniques with practices like yoga, meditation, and nutrition to promote overall well-being. This reflects a broader understanding that mental health is deeply connected to physical health and lifestyle choices.

These emerging trends in psychology highlight the field's adaptability and its ability to respond to the changing needs of society. As technology advances, social dynamics shift, and new discoveries about the brain come to light, psychology continues to evolve, offering new ways to improve mental health and enrich human experience.

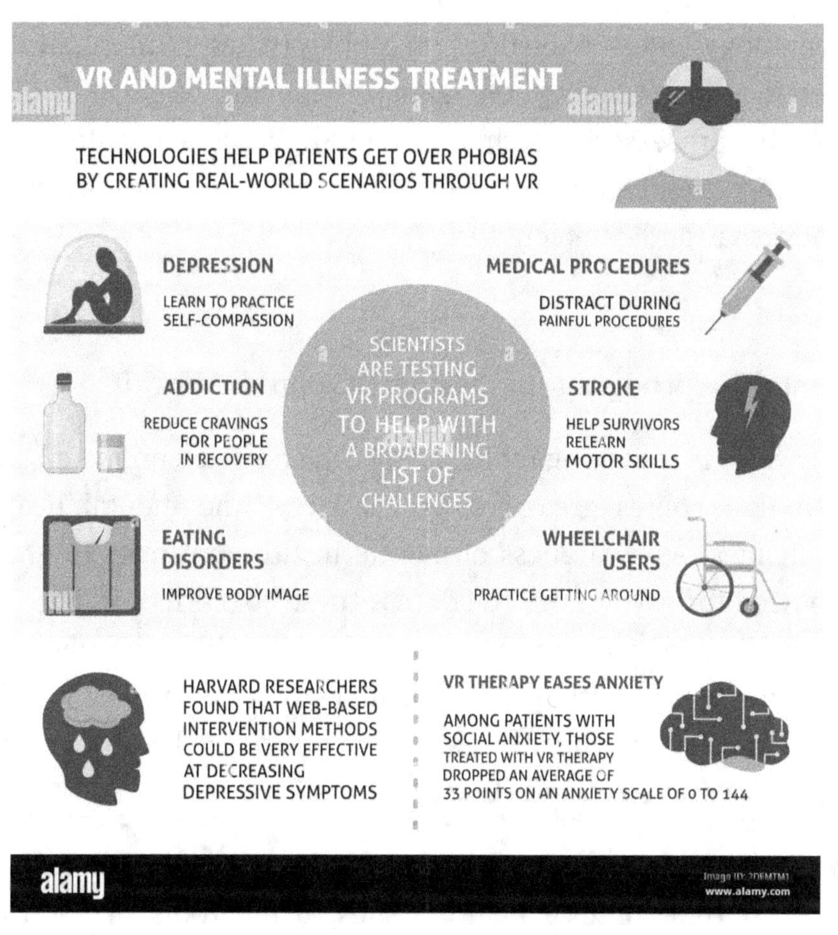

The Future of Psychology and Technology. Source: alamy.com

The Importance of Psychology in the Future

As the world continues to change, psychology will play an even more vital role in shaping how we adapt, grow, and thrive. The challenges we face in the future—whether they're related to technology, mental health, or global issues—will require a deeper understanding of human behavior, emotions, and thought processes. Psychology will help us navigate these challenges and create a future that's more compassionate, innovative, and connected.

Mental Health in an Increasingly Complex World

The world is becoming more fast-paced and interconnected, but with that comes greater stress, anxiety, and mental health challenges. As awareness of mental health continues to grow, the need for psychology to address these concerns will become even more critical. Future psychologists will not only help individuals cope with personal challenges but also contribute to improving mental health systems at a broader level, ensuring more accessible and effective care for all.

With advances in technology, psychologists will explore new ways to treat mental health issues, using tools like virtual therapy, apps, and even artificial intelligence. These advancements will help people access support wherever they are, breaking down barriers and making mental health care more available and personalized.

The Role of Psychology in Technological Advancements

Technology is reshaping nearly every aspect of our lives, and psychology is key to understanding how these changes affect us. As artificial intelligence, robotics, and virtual reality become more integrated into daily life, psychology will help us comprehend their impact on human behavior and relationships. Psychologists will study how we interact with machines, how technology changes the way we think, and how we can use these tools to improve our well-being.

For instance, as workplaces become more automated and reliant on technology, psychologists will need to help individuals adapt to new roles and responsibilities, ensuring that the human element remains central in an increasingly digital world.

Addressing Global Challenges

From climate change to social inequality, the future will bring complex global challenges that require collective action. Psychology will play a critical role in understanding how people can come together to address these issues. By studying behavior on a societal level, psychologists will help identify what motivates individuals to take action, how communities can collaborate more effectively, and what barriers prevent meaningful change.

Psychology will also be crucial in fostering resilience as people face environmental changes, economic uncertainty, and other global crises. The ability to adapt, cope, and find hope in difficult times will be a key focus for psychologists, helping individuals and communities stay strong in the face of adversity.

The Evolution of Human Connection

While technology connects us like never before, it can also create distance in our personal relationships. As we increasingly rely on digital communication, psychology will be essential in helping us understand how to maintain meaningful connections and navigate the complexities of online relationships. Psychologists will explore how social media affects our sense of self, how we form and sustain relationships in a virtual world, and what new forms of community and belonging might emerge in the future.

In a world that is always evolving, psychology offers a framework to understand not just where we've come from, but where we are going. The future will demand greater insight into human behavior, and psychology will continue to be a crucial tool for shaping a world that values well-being, connection, and growth.

Your Role in the Science of You

Psychology is often seen as something external—a field of study for experts, researchers, and therapists. But at its core, psychology is about understanding *you*—your thoughts, emotions, and behaviors. And you play a central role in this journey of self-discovery. The science of psychology can offer valuable insights, but it's your willingness to explore, reflect, and apply those insights that makes all the difference.

Taking Ownership of Your Mind

The first step in becoming active in the science of you is taking ownership of your mind. This means recognizing that your thoughts and feelings are not just random events happening to you; they are deeply connected to the choices you make, your past experiences, and your environment. While it's easy to feel like you're at the mercy of your emotions or circumstances, psychology shows us that we have more control than we might think.

By paying attention to your inner world—your thoughts, feelings, and reactions—you begin to understand patterns in your behavior. Are there situations that consistently trigger stress or frustration? Do certain thoughts keep you stuck in a cycle of self-doubt? Being mindful of these patterns allows you to take the first step toward positive change. With awareness comes the power to choose how you respond, rather than simply reacting out of habit.

Becoming a Student of Yourself

One of the most empowering things you can do is to approach your own mind like a student eager to learn. This doesn't mean obsessively analyzing everything you do, but rather being curious about why you think, feel, and act the way you do. When you treat yourself as a student of psychology, you begin to uncover the hidden influences that shape your life.

For example, you might start by exploring your beliefs—about yourself, others, and the world. Where did those beliefs come from? Are they serving you, or are they holding you back? By asking these questions, you begin to unravel the layers of conditioning that influence your everyday behavior.

Psychology offers tools to help you in this process, from techniques in cognitive behavioral therapy (CBT) that challenge unhelpful thoughts to mindfulness practices that keep you grounded in the present moment. These tools can become part of your personal toolkit, helping you navigate life with more clarity and purpose.

The Power of Self-Reflection

Self-reflection is a powerful practice that allows you to check in with yourself, understand your motivations, and make conscious adjustments to how you live. Through regular reflection, whether it's journaling, meditation, or simply taking time to think, you can deepen your self-awareness.

Ask yourself questions like: *What am I feeling right now? Why did I react that way in that situation? What can I learn from this experience?* These questions invite you to look inward and learn more about yourself, leading to personal growth and transformation.

Self-reflection also helps you stay connected to your goals and values. It's easy to get caught up in the day-to-day demands of life and lose sight of what really matters. By pausing to reflect, you can realign your actions with your deeper sense of purpose, ensuring that you're not just living on autopilot, but making intentional choices that contribute to your well-being.

Applying Psychological Insights to Everyday Life

The science of psychology isn't just something to be studied— it's something to be lived. Once you understand the principles behind how the mind works, you can apply them to improve your everyday life. This might involve using relaxation techniques to manage stress, developing healthier communication skills in your relationships, or practicing positive thinking to shift your mindset.

It's important to remember that change takes time. Personal growth is a process, and it's normal to face setbacks along the way. But with the insights from psychology, you have a roadmap to guide you. By applying what you learn about yourself and being patient with the process, you can create meaningful, lasting changes in your life.

Creating Your Own Path

Ultimately, the science of you is about creating your own path. Psychology gives you the tools, but you are the one who decides how to use them. You get to choose how you want to grow, what goals you want to pursue, and how you want to live. This is your journey.

Embrace the role of being both the scientist and the subject of your own life. Be curious, be compassionate with yourself, and be open to change. As you continue to explore the depths of your own mind, remember that the science of you is ongoing—there is always more to learn, and with that learning comes the opportunity to live a more fulfilling, intentional, and authentic life.

Conclusion

Throughout this book, we've explored the fascinating world of psychology and uncovered the science of you. We've taken a journey through the core areas of psychology—understanding how our minds work, how we form relationships, and how we can make meaningful choices in our lives. From the study of cognitive processes to the power of emotions, from our personal identity to the social influences that shape us, psychology offers us a deeper understanding of what it means to be human.

At the heart of it all is the idea that psychology isn't just about academic theories or complex experiments. It's about practical, everyday insights that can help you live a more intentional, empowered life. Whether it's managing stress, building better habits, improving your relationships, or simply understanding yourself better, the lessons of psychology are tools you can use to thrive.

The message of this book is simple, yet powerful: by understanding how your mind works, you gain the ability to shape your life with greater awareness and purpose. You're not at the mercy of unconscious drives or outside influences—you have the knowledge and power to change, grow, and build the life you want.

As you move forward, remember that psychology is a lifelong journey. The insights you've gained here are just the beginning. Keep exploring, keep questioning, and most importantly, keep applying what you've learned. Your mind is your greatest asset, and the more you understand it, the more control you have over your experiences and choices.

In the end, psychology is about understanding yourself and the world around you. By using these insights, you can live a life that is not only more fulfilling but also more connected to others. The power of psychology lies in its ability to help us lead lives that are not only smarter, but also kinder, more resilient, and deeply meaningful.

So, take what you've learned and go forward with curiosity and confidence. Use psychology as your guide to navigate the complexities of life, and remember that every small step you take toward understanding yourself is a step toward living a richer, more intentional life.

Dear Reader,

I hope you found the book insightful and valuable.

Your feedback is invaluable to me. If you enjoyed reading this book, I would appreciate it if you could take a moment to leave a review on the reading apps and platforms.

Thank you for your support, and I wish you all the best.

Kind regards,
Ghazwan

About the Author

Ghazwan is a passionate entrepreneur and business strategist dedicated to helping individuals and organizations achieve their full potential with a deep understanding of modern businesses' challenges and opportunities.

With a Master's degree in Computer and Systems Sciences from Stockholm University, specializing in eService design, requirement engineering, and business process management, he is equipped to innovate cutting-edge solutions.

He believes in the power of collaboration and lifelong learning, and his mission is to empower people to reach their goals and positively impact the world.